Building Bible Character

By Joe Price

© **Truth Publications, Inc. 2024. Second Printing.** All rights reserved. No part of this book may be reproduced in any form without prior written permission from the publisher. Printed in the United States of America.

ISBN 10: 1-58427-240-6

ISBN 13: 978-1-58427-240-3

First Printing: 2008

All photos and graphics are from istockphoto.com.

Truth Publications, Inc.
CEI Bookstore
220 S. Marion St., Athens, AL 35611
855-492-6657
sales@truthpublications.com
www.truthbooks.com

Table of Contents

Lesson 1:   Conversion to Christ 5

Lesson 2:   Young People Can Build Bible Character 10

Lesson 3:   The Example of Jesus 15

Lesson 4:   Flee Youthful Lusts 20

Lesson 5:   Pursue Righteousness 25

Lesson 6:   Pursue Faith 31

Lesson 7:   Pursue Love 37

Lesson 8:   Pursue Peace 43

Lesson 9:   A Pure Heart 49

Lesson 10: Sound Speech 55

Lesson 11: Self-Control 60

Lesson 12: Moral Courage 66

Lesson 13: Self-Sacrifice 72

Lesson 1

Conversion to Christ

Introduction

The world needs young men and women of character, young people who are not afraid to live their faith in the face of a faithless society.

Even worldly people generally have some idea of and appreciation for personal character. Christians are not the only people who regard such character traits as honor, integrity, and fairness. But, like so many other things, man's definition of character falls far short of the divine ideal.

Christian character rises above the world's accepted norms. For example, while the world admires the benefits of love, it rarely advocates the love of one's enemies (Matt. 5:43). Only when we allow the Bible, the word of God, to define and explain character will we be able to build the kind of character that pleases God.

What Is Character?

The English word "character" comes from a Latin word which means, "mark, distinctive quality" and from a Greek word meaning "to scratch, engrave" (*Merriam-Webster Dictionary; Online Etymology Dictionary*). So, one's character consists of the distinctive marks or traits that are etched or engraved on a person's heart. Character includes the morals and ethics that define a person. The Bible puts it this way: "For as he thinks in his heart, so is he" (Prov. 23:7).

Bible Character Defines the Person

A person's words and actions express his character. It has been said that character is not *what* a person does but *who* a person is. More precisely, character is whom a person is (or chooses to be) when no one is watching! D. L. Moody aptly observed that "character is what a man is in the dark."

We are reminded of the teenager Joseph who, although being violently removed from every familiar surrounding of his young life (family and friends), consistently kept his faith in God and would not sin—even when it cost him his job, his reputation, and his freedom (Gen. 37 and 39). Joseph was a young man of character. He knew that God was always watching and seeing how he lived. His desire was to please God, not man (2 Cor. 5:9).

In Proverbs 3:1-12 a wise father gave guidance and instruction to his son about the importance and blessings of godly character. Notice how many times he talked about the heart in this passage. This constant emphasis on the heart reminds us that unless we mold our heart into what God wants it to be our attempt to build Bible character will be pointless. The heart is the place we must start if we wish to succeed in building Bible character.

Qualities & Results of Godly Character (Prov. 3:1-12)

Comes from the Heart
- Obedience, 3:1-2
- Mercy & truth, 3:3
- Faith in God, 3:5
- Consider God, 3:6
- Depart from evil, 3:7
- Honor God, 3:9
- Accept divine discipline, 3:11

Blessings Obtained
- Life & peace, 3:2
- Favor, & understanding, 3:4
- Divine guidance, 3:6
- Strength, 3:8
- Plenty, 3:10
- God's love, 3:12

Our Model for Bible Character Is Jesus

Lesson Three will consider the example of Jesus that helps us build our character. For now it is important to understand that Jesus is our ultimate model for building Bible character. "A disciple is not above his teacher, but everyone who is perfectly trained will be like his teacher" (Luke 6:40). The goal of every disciple is to learn and live the will of his Master. Every Christian should desire his character to be like Christ. The gospel forms Christ in us, and we have a sure "hope of glory" (Gal. 4:19; Col. 1:27).

Building Bible Character Begins with Conversion to Christ

To speak of Christ being "in" a person, as well as of that person being "in Christ," is to describe the relationship that is established when the sinner is saved from his sins. "For as many of you as were baptized into Christ have put on Christ" (Gal. 3:27). When a lost believer repents and is baptized into Christ he is saved from his sins and enters a saved relationship with Christ. "Therefore, if anyone is in Christ, he is a new creature; old things have passed away; behold, all things have become new" (2 Cor. 5:17). Being in this new relationship with Christ, the Christian is a disciple of Christ (a learner and follower of Jesus). Now that he is "in Christ" he is no longer to live in and for sin, but "in Christ" and for Christ (Rom. 6:1-11).

Building Bible character begins with becoming a Christian. Disciples train themselves to be like their Master. Since it is Christians who are disciples of Jesus, one must first be a Christian in order to develop character that is like the Master (Acts 11:26; Luke 6:40). If you want to build Bible character, begin by becoming a Christian, a disciple of Christ.

Building Blocks of Bible Character: Colossians 3:1-17

Colossians 3:1-17 gives us the building blocks we need to develop Christ-like character. This passage teaches us *how* to build Bible character.

When one is baptized into Christ he is "raised with Christ" by the power of God from the death of sin into newness of life (Col. 3:1; 2:12; Rom. 6:4). To build Bible character, once a person has become a Christian, he must (1) *Seek* things that are above (Col. 3:1); (2) *Set* his mind on heavenly things (Col. 3:2); and (3) *Sustain* a faithful life with Christ (Col. 3:3).

A new approach to sin is necessary in order to build a new character in Christ: sin must be put to death (Col. 3:5-11). We cannot continue to live in past sins and expect God to bless us. We must cease sin, whether it is the sensual desires of the flesh (3:5-7) or the attitudes and actions that hurt others (3:8-9); we must put off the old man of sin and put on the new man that is like Christ (3:10-11).

A new heart is necessary in order to develop this new approach to sin (Col. 3:12-15). Just as in Proverbs 23:7, the gospel teaches, "a good man out of the good treasure of his heart brings forth good things, and an evil man out of the evil treasure brings forth evil things" (Matt. 12:35). Only as we put on a new heart will we also put off sin. Character building involves rebuilding our heart so that we think, feel, and act like Christ.

A new message must dwell in one's heart to truly build a new heart (Col. 3:16). The word of Christ must be implanted deeply within one's heart in order to build a character that is like Christ (Jas. 1:21-25).

A new authority must be respected and honored in all we say and do in order to let the word of Christ dwell in our heart. "And whatever you do in word or deed, do all in the name of the Lord Jesus, giving thanks to God the Father through Him" (Col. 3:17).

Building Bible character will help us choose to have new conduct in all of our relationships with others (Col. 3:18-4:2).

Here then, are the building blocks of Bible character: The authority of Christ expressed in the word of Christ, along with a new heart that forms a new approach toward sin and righteousness in our life. When the authority of Christ is respected and His word is obeyed in all things, the heart is renewed after the image of Christ and sin will be consistently and consciously put away from one's life. Stated another way, as we grow and mature in Christ we will be building godly character that pleases God.

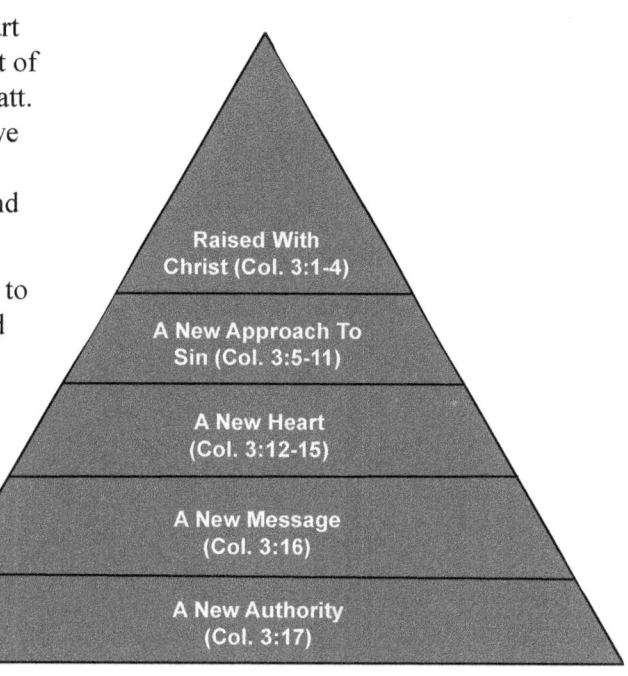

The Faithful Endurance of Bible Character

Possessing Bible character is a sign of strength, not weakness. It is the inner strength of faith that stands fast in the face of adversity, trial, and temptation. The apostle Paul assures us that, when a Christian's faith is tested and he patiently endures, "approved character" results (Rom. 5:3-4).

When your faith is put to the test at school, at home or on the job, remember these words from the wise man Solomon: "The integrity of the upright will guide them, but the perversity of the unfaithful will destroy them" (Prov. 11:3).

Questions

True or False

_____ 1. It takes courage to have Bible character today.

_____ 2. Character is what others say about you.

_____ 3. As a man feels in his heart, so is he.

_____ 4. A disciple is not above his teacher.

_____ 5. Becoming a Christian is the way to begin building Bible character.

_____ 6. When a person is a Christian he does not have to work at overcoming sin.

_____ 7. Bible character is built on respecting the authority of Christ.

Questions for Discussion

1. What is character? Why is it important to build Bible character? _____

   _____

   _____

2. How does the Christian's character rise above the general view of character? Give an example.

   _____

   _____

3. Name some qualities of faith that are needed in order to build Bible character (2 Cor. 5:7; Heb. 11; Rom. 5:3-4). _____

   _____

   _____

4. What people, places and things was Joseph taken away from that could have made it easy for him to abandon his faith in God? How did he show his character in Genesis 39:1-20? _____

   _____

   _____

5. What does it mean to be a disciple? What is the goal of the disciple of Jesus (Luke 6:40)? _____

   _____

   _____

6. What does it mean to have Christ "in" you (Gal. 4:19; Col. 1:27)? _____

   _____

   _____

How is Christ formed in you? _____
_____
_____

7. According to Proverbs 3:1-12, what kind of heart should we develop? _____
_____

   What will be the result? _____
_____

8. Name some ways you can show mercy and kindness to others (Prov. 3:3). _____
_____
_____

9. Name the three things Christians must do that are stated in Colossians 3:1-3. _____
_____
_____
_____

10. What is the wrath of God? _____

    Upon whom does it come (Col. 3:6)? _____
_____

11. What must be allowed to dwell in one's heart? _____

    Explain why this is necessary in order to develop a new heart (that is like Christ) (Col. 3:12-16).
_____
_____

12. Discuss how you can show godly character in your relationship with your parents; with your classmates at school; on the job. Include examples (Col. 3:18-4:1). _____
_____
_____
_____

Lesson 2

Young People Can Build Bible Character

> **An Example to Believers**
> 1 Timothy 4:12
> - In word (Tit. 2:7-8)
> - In conduct (1 Pet. 1:11-12)
> - In love (1 John 4:19-21; John 13:34-35)
> - In spirit (Rom. 8:5-8)
> - In faith (1 Thess. 1:3)
> - In purity (1 Tim. 6:11; 2 Tim. 2:22)

Introduction

Unquestionably the youth of today face many moral choices: Alcohol, drugs, sex, crime, and the pressure of social acceptance by others are just some of the moral issues young people face. As a young person standing on the threshold of adulthood, the decisions you make will shape your life now as well as eternally.

The judgment you use and the choices you make as a teenager will likely stay with you for the rest of your life. "How important is getting an education? What kind of person should I date? What kind of person do I intend to marry? Do I want to get married? Will I try drugs? Will I engage in premarital sex? Will I attend the junior high or high school dance? Will I join my friends when they want to go to the drinking party? What kind of clothes will I wear?" Get the picture? The decisions you are making now have far-reaching consequences. The choices you make reflect your outlook on life, your faith, your morality, and the values you hold.

All of these decisions (and more) will be based on whether you decide to be a disciple of Jesus and build the kind of character He wants you to have (Luke 6:40). The first decision you must make is to be a Christian and to live a moral, godly life (Josh. 24:15; Matt. 6:33). The decision to live in a way that pleases God is of first importance, because it will help you see more clearly the other choices you will need to make to follow Him (Luke 9:23).

The Challenges of Youth

Some will try to convince you that it is neither possible nor necessary for young people to build Bible character and live godly lives. Friends will say such things as, "You are only young once! Do what you want to while you can! Don't be a spoil-sport, have some fun!" Those who do not care about the will of God and godly living will try to persuade you to live for yourself, for the here and now, without being concerned about moral and spiritual matters. They say you can think about God *after* you have finished "living it up." They will try to convince you that you cannot enjoy life and be a Christian, too.

What they do not tell you is this: "Do not be deceived, God is not mocked; for whatever a man sows, that he will also reap. For he who sows to his flesh will of the flesh reap corruption, but he who sows to the Spirit will of the Spirit reap everlasting life" (Gal. 6:7-8). They do not tell you

> **Three "R's" of Youth**
> Eccl. 11:9-12:1
> - Rejoice in your youth (11:9)
> - Remove sorrow from your heart (11:10)
> - Remember now your Creator in the days of your youth (12:1)

that life is uncertain and can be taken away in an instant (Jas. 4:13-15; Heb. 9:27). They do not tell you about the judgment day when we will each stand before God and our life is judged (2 Cor. 5:10).

Being young presents special challenges. For instance, the word of God warns of "youthful lusts" (2 Tim. 2:22). God provides ways of escape so temptation can be resisted (1 Cor. 10:13). Some may despise you because you are young (1 Tim. 4:12). The very fact that one is young means he or she has not yet had many of the experiences of life that come with age (Job 32:2-7; 1 Kings 3:7-12). But, the word of God will light your path so you can grow in knowledge and wisdom (Psa. 119:9, 105; Prov. 6:23). The word of God gives strength to youth: "I have written to you, young men, because you are strong, and the word of God abides in you, and you have overcome the wicked one" (1 John 2:14).

The Possibility of Building Character in Youth

The Bible does not assign a specific age when one becomes accountable before God. When a young person develops the capacity to know right and wrong and begins to make conscious decisions based on that knowledge, God holds him or her accountable (Rom. 7:7-10).

Building godly character does not mean one no longer has any natural desires. It does mean one deliberately decides to control his or her desires in order to reflect godliness and holiness (Rom. 8:13; 1 Pet. 1:13-16). The person with Bible character puts off the old man of sin and puts on the new man (2 Cor. 5:17; Eph. 4:17-24; Col. 3:9-10). To build Bible character we must crucify self (Gal. 2:20). "Me, myself, and I" is no longer in charge; Christ Jesus is now the Master.

The person who is living by faith determines no longer to allow sin to rule and dominate his life: "knowing this, that our old man was crucified with Him, that the body of sin might be done away with, that we should no longer be slaves of sin" (Rom. 6:6). Whether young or old, the Christian views himself as dead to sin and alive to God (Rom. 6:11). He is now a servant of righteousness instead of being a slave of sin (Rom. 6:15-18).

Building godly character does not mean a perverted denial of everything in life. It does mean choosing the things in this life that enhance the joys of righteousness: "He has shown you, O man, what is good; and what does the LORD require of you but to do justly, to love mercy, and to walk humbly with your God?" (Mic. 6:8).

> **Everyone chooses to live by some moral standard; everyone serves some master.**

God gave us life so we can walk with Him and enjoy the pleasures He provides us (Eccl. 2:24; 3:12-13; 5:18-19; 8:14-15; 9:9-10; 12:13). The wise man Solomon gave inspired counsel to young people in Ecclesiastes 11:9-12:1. There, young people are advised to *rejoice* in youth, *remove* evil and *remember* God.

1. Rejoice in your youth. The strength and vitality of youth are gifts from God (Prov. 20:29). The world is before you, and God wants you to enjoy it: "... let your heart cheer you in the days of your youth; Walk in the ways of your heart, And in the sight of your eyes" (Eccl. 11:9). Like any other blessing, the vitality of youth comes with responsibility: "But know that for all these God will bring you into judgment." You have great potential to achieve great things. While pursuing your dreams and ambitions in life, keep in mind that every one will be brought into account by God.

2. Remove sorrow from your heart. Life will bring its share of trials and sorrow regardless of how long we live (Psa. 90:10). Because youth is short-lived ("childhood and youth are vanity"), Solomon recommends a path that will lessen the likelihood of exasperation and dissatisfaction in life. By putting away evil you will be choosing a life of contentment without regret.

3. Remember now your Creator. There is no better time than youth to believe and obey God. It is wise to understand that, as you grow older, there will be more and more distractions that can draw you away from God. Better to establish a pattern of faithful service to God while you are young than to think that "after I live the way I want to" I will do God's will. The fact is, you do not know how long you are going to live (Jas. 4:14). It is foolish to think one's heart will not harden over years and years of neglect and disobedience (Heb. 3:7-14).

Building godly character means making a definite choice to live by faith and reject sin. Everyone chooses to live by some moral standard; everyone serves some master (Rom. 6:12-14; Josh. 24:15; Matt. 6:24). And, everyone will reap the harvest of his or her choice, whether the result is good or bad (Gal. 6:7-8; 2 Cor. 5:10). The person who chooses to live in sin will die in his sin (Ezek. 18:20; Rom. 6:23). The person who chooses to live in obedient faith will obtain eternal life (Rom. 6:15-23).

Some want to blame God for the sin (with its sorrow) they have chosen. They do this by saying things like, "It's too hard not to sin," or "God made me this way, so if I sin it must be His fault!" But, James warns us not to be deceived by such worldly thinking (Jas. 1:16). "Let no one say when he is tempted, 'I am

tempted by God'; for God cannot be tempted by evil, nor does He Himself tempt anyone" (Jas. 1:13).

Godly character will compel us to look for and make choices in life that resist temptation and reject sin. By so doing one will receive the crown of life the Lord has promised to those who love Him (Jas. 1:12).

The Choice of Godly Character

God assures us that one will be blessed when he chooses to say "no" to sin's enticements and "yes" to doing God's will: "Blessed is the man who walks not in the counsel of the ungodly, nor stands in the path of sinners, nor sits in the seat of the scornful; But his delight is in the law of the LORD, and in His law he meditates day and night" (Psa. 1:1-2).

Building Bible character is demanding. Sacrifice is always required to follow Jesus

(Matt. 10:34-39). The cost of character may be the loss of friends, the support of family, the denial of pleasure, or even the giving up of one's life (Luke 14:25-33). The person who is willing to renounce all that he has or is in order to follow Jesus is the person who, by paying the price of discipleship, builds godly character.

Building Bible character lays up treasure in heaven. Our earthly existence is uncertain and brief (Jas. 4:13-14). Therefore we ought to say, "If the Lord wills, we shall live and do this or that" (Jas. 4:15). Laying up treasures in heaven is far more important than laying up earthly wealth, power or pleasure (Matt. 6:19-21). By choosing to build godly character you are laying up treasures in heaven.

Building Bible character shows the wisdom of obeying Jesus Christ. Jesus is the author (cause) of eternal salvation to all who obey Him (Heb. 5:9). Jesus said the person who hears and obeys His teachings is wise, while those who hear Him but do not obey Him are foolish (Matt. 7:24-27). Possessing the character to say "yes" to Christ and "no" to man is essential to building Bible character.

Building Bible character reflects eternal values. Like the runner who strives to win the race, the Christian must be dedicated to heaven's prize of eternal life. Unlike the athlete, though, the Christian "runs" to obtain an "imperishable" crown (1 Cor. 9:24-27; cf. 2 Tim. 4:7-8).

Young people can live godly lives. Young people can build Bible character. The word of God advises a course of life for youth that will bring happiness now and eternal life beyond the grave.

Questions

True or False

_____ 1. The choices you make do not say anything about the kind of person you are.

_____ 2. Our moral choices do not have any consequences.

_____ 3. The most important decision one should make is becoming a Christian.

_____ 4. It is impossible for a young person to live godly.

_____ 5. Teenagers will not die.

_____ 6. We sin because God made us this way.

_____ 7. It is easy to remember God when you are old.

Questions for Discussion

1. Discuss whether young people today face different choices than young people in Bible times. ___

   _____

   _____

2. Name some excuses given for why young people do not have to build Bible character. _____

   _____

3. Why do you think those who do not obey God try to persuade others to join them in sin (John 3:19-21; Prov. 1:10-19)? _____

   _____

4. What is the "age of accountability"? _____
   _____
   Is it the same for every person (Rom. 7:7-10)? _____

5. What does it mean to "deny" self (Luke 9:23)? _____
   Name some specific ways of doing this. _____
   _____

6. How can someone "despise your youth"? How can you help prevent this from happening (1 Tim. 4:12)? _____
   _____

7. Discuss what it means to "remove sorrow from your heart" and how to do so (Eccl. 11:10). ____
   _____
   _____

8. According to James 4:13-14, what two things should we always remember about life? _____
   _____
   Because of these two things, how should we approach life (Jas. 4:15)? _____
   _____

9. What is the "old man" of sin? _____
   What must be done to it in order to build Bible character? _____
   _____
   How is this accomplished (Eph. 4:20-24; Col. 3:9-10; Rom. 6:6-18)? _____
   _____
   _____

10. How do we show ourselves to be foolish or wise in life (Matt. 7:24-27)? _____
    _____
    _____

11. What is laid up in heaven for those who love the Lord's appearing? _____
    How is it obtained (2 Tim. 4:7-8; 1 Cor. 9:24-27)? _____
    _____
    _____

Lesson 3

The Example of Jesus

Introduction

It has been said, "The man who makes a character makes foes" (Edward Young). This was certainly true in the case of Jesus of Nazareth. Although his life was filled with doing good and teaching righteousness, he was hated and killed: "If I had not done among them the works which no one else did, they would have no sin; but now they have seen and also hated both Me and My Father" (John 15:24; Acts 10:38).

Before his death, Jesus assured his apostles, "If the world hates you, you know that it hated me before it hated you" (John 15:18). The same is true today of those who choose to be disciples of Jesus: "A disciple is not above his teacher, but everyone who is perfectly trained will be like his teacher" (Luke 6:40).

The character we choose to build and to live by speaks volumes concerning whether we love the light of truth or prefer the darkness of evil. "And this is the condemnation, that the light has come into the world, and men loved darkness rather than light, because their deeds were evil. For everyone practicing evil hates the light and does not come to the light, lest his deeds should be exposed. But he who does the truth comes to the light, that his deeds may be clearly seen, that they have been done in God" (John 3:19-21).

Conformed to the Image of Christ

It is God's will that Christians be "conformed to the image of His Son" (Rom. 8:29). We are to be fashioned into his likeness. We are to imitate Jesus in our character and conduct. Christ dwells in our hearts through faith, so that we no longer live for ourselves, but for him (Eph. 3:17; Gal. 2:20).

Jesus expects us to build our character according to the light of His revealed truth. And, he has set the example of character for us to follow. The life of Jesus shows that young people can develop a character that pleases God even though it will antagonize those who live in the darkness of sin. As a youth, Jesus maintained a spotless character and lived without sin (1 Pet. 2:22). Although we have sinned and fallen short of God's glory, Jesus is the model we must follow to shape and mold ourselves into his image. Our attitude, values, goals and aspirations, and conduct should be built after the model our Teacher has set before us (Luke 6:40).

Jesus: Model of Humility

Jesus Christ, who is Immanuel ("God with us"), is the model of humility for us all. "Let this mind be in you which was also in Christ Jesus, who, being in the form of God, did not consider it robbery to be equal with God, but made Himself of no reputation, taking the form of a bondservant, and coming in the likeness of men. And being found in appearance as a man, He humbled Himself and became obedient to the point of death, even the death of the cross" (Phil. 2:5-8).

Jesus entered this world in modest surroundings. His first breath of life was drawn from a feeding trough for livestock (Luke 2:7). His parents were common people of modest means who lived in the small and insignificant village of Nazareth in Galilee (Luke 2:39). To be a Nazarene was to be viewed with disdain as one of no consequence: "Can anything good come out of Nazareth?" (John 1:46; Matt. 2:23). Instead of growing up to resent his humble way of life, humility became a defining trait of his character.

As a boy growing up in Nazareth, Jesus lived a humble life as a carpenter's son (Matt. 13:55). As a young boy he lived in such a way that others saw his good character and conduct. "And the Child grew and became strong in spirit, filled with wisdom; and the grace of God was upon Him" (Luke 2:40). The boy Jesus brought favor and delight to the people around Him (Luke 2:52). He was not arrogant or rude in His behavior, but respectful toward His elders (Lev. 19:32).

Jesus had brothers and sisters (Matt. 13:55). Living with siblings presents challenges to one's character. There will be disagreements and differences that arise. Learning to share and work together is an important part of growing up with brothers and sisters. Jesus learned and lived these lessons, setting an example of cooperation worthy for us to follow.

Jesus: Model of Obedience

In the development of character, young people must learn to overcome selfishness. It is common to see young people who act as if everything should revolve around them, that they should always have their own way, and that people should always do what we want. Although we are not given a great deal of information about the early life of Jesus, what is recorded reveals a boy who was humble, respectful, and unselfish, as well as obedient to His parents and to God.

From an early age, Jesus was committed to doing the will of God. When Jesus was twelve years old he went with his family to Jerusalem to observe the Passover (Luke 2:41-42). When the feast concluded His parents began the journey home thinking Jesus was with family and friends. When they could not find Him they returned to Jerusalem where they spent three days looking for Him, finding Him in the temple. Jesus was sitting among the teachers of the law of God, listening and asking them questions. He had an intense interest in the law of God. He said He "must be about my father's business" when His mother told Him of their anxious search for Him (Luke 2:43-48).

Wisdom is shown by the child who learns early in life to live under the restraints and directives of law (Prov. 28:7). Jesus was devoted to God's law, an example that every young person can imitate. "But seek first the kingdom of God and His righteousness, and all these things shall be added to you" (Matt. 6:33).

A child is to honor his or her parents by obeying them (Eph. 6:1-3).

> **A child is to honor his or her parents by obeying them (Eph. 6:1-3). Jesus set this example by obeying His parents. Even when your parents do not understand you, God expects you to be respectful and obedient to them.**

Jesus set this example by obeying His parents. Even when your parents do not understand you, God expects you to be respectful and obedient to them. Although Joseph and Mary "did not understand the statement which He spoke to them," Jesus "went down with them and came to Nazareth, and was subject to them" (Luke 2:50-51).

Jesus: Model of Honest Labor

Jesus was known as "the carpenter," having learned and followed the family tradition of Joseph (Mark 6:3). A carpenter not only helped build houses, but, depending on the skill achieved, the furniture that went inside them. Carts and wagons and other items made of wood were the common products of carpenters of that day. To be a good carpenter one had to learn to use many different tools. To learn any trade requires self-discipline and consistent effort. From an early age, Jesus must have seen His father work to provide for His family. Young Jesus saw Joseph's hard work, and throughout His life, Jesus displayed a work ethic of sincere integrity and effort. Jesus expects all who have a job to draw on a character of honesty and devotion to accomplish their work (Eph. 6:5-8; Col. 3:22-25).

Jesus: Model of Personal Growth

The Scripture says that as He grew up in Nazareth, "Jesus increased in wisdom and stature, and in favor with God and men" (Luke 2:52). While growing up we are confident Jesus experienced the things most young people encounter. As Jesus progressed through childhood to adolescence and into adulthood He faced the challenges that young people continue to confront: choosing friends, establishing values, developing character. We are certain that Jesus resisted youthful lusts and pursued holiness (2 Tim. 2:22; 1 Tim. 6:11). He developed His moral character to reflect godliness and righteousness. We are confident He learned the word of God as His parents taught him from God's law (Deut. 6:4-9; 11:18-19). Jesus went into the synagogue on the Sabbath where the law and the prophets were read, thereby establishing a pattern of learning and listening to the word of God (Luke 4:16).

> **Jesus Grew Up**
> **Luke 2:52**
> - Mentally (in wisdom)
> - Physically (in stature)
> - Spiritually (in favor with God)
> - Socially (in favor with men)

In every part of His life from childhood to adulthood, Jesus set an example that helps young people build godly character in an ungodly world.

NOTES

Questions

True or False

___ 1. True disciples pattern themselves after their master (Luke 6:40).
___ 2. Everybody will like us when we model our character after Jesus (John 15:18).
___ 3. The Christian does not have to try to be like Christ in his life (Rom. 8:29).
___ 4. Immanuel means "Man with God" (Matt. 1:23).
___ 5. To be from Nazareth meant that people thought highly of you (John 1:46).
___ 6. God's favor was with Jesus as He grew up (Luke 2:40).
___ 7. Jesus did not have any brothers and sisters (Matt. 13:55).
___ 8. Jesus disobeyed His parents when he remained in Jerusalem after the Passover (Luke 2:41-50).
___ 9. Jesus learned the value of work as a carpenter (Mark 6:3).
___ 10. Jesus regularly went to the synagogue on the Sabbath day where the Scriptures were read (Luke 4:16-19).

Questions for Discussion

1. Why did some people hate Jesus? _____

   _____

   Will they hate you for following Jesus? _____

   Is this a good reason not to follow Jesus (John 15:24, 18)? _____

2. Who is the Christian supposed to be like? _____

   In what ways are we to be like Him (Luke 6:40; 1 Pet. 2:21; Gal. 2:20)? _____

   _____

   _____

3. How does Christ live in our hearts (Eph. 3:17)? _____

   _____

   _____

4. What is humility? _____

   _____

   Discuss the humility of Jesus in the light of Philippians 2:5-8 and John 1:1-3. Give examples of His humble life. _____

   _____

   _____

The Example of Jesus

5. Name some ways that Jesus honored His father and mother. _____
   _____
   _____

6. What can you do to honor your parents? _____
   _____
   _____

7. How do you know Jesus was not a lazy youth? _____
   _____
   _____

8. What was a synagogue? _____
   What was done there every week (Luke 4:16-19)? _____
   _____
   _____

9. Tell what Jesus was doing in the temple when He was twelve years old. What passage of Scripture tells about it? _____
   _____
   _____

10. What can parents do to help their children build godly character? _____
    _____
    _____

11. What can you do to become more like Jesus when He was growing up?
    _____
    _____
    _____

Lesson 4

Flee Youthful Lusts

Introduction

The goal of building Bible character is not completed in a day or a year; it is the expression of one's faith that lasts a lifetime. The first century Greek essayist Plutarch observed that "character is simply habit long continued" (*Morals*). At about the same period of human history, the Holy Spirit inspired the apostle of Christ to say,

> Not that I have already attained, or am already perfected; but I press on, that I may lay hold of that for which Christ Jesus has also laid hold of me. Brethren, I do not count myself to have apprehended; but one thing I do, forgetting those things which are behind and reaching forward to those things which are ahead, I press toward the goal for the prize of the upward call of God in Christ Jesus (Phil. 3:12-14).

There are obstacles we have to overcome to successfully build our character into what Christ wants us to be. Our adversary, the devil, is always trying to prevent us from being faithful to Jesus (1 Pet. 5:8). By identifying the dangers and hindrances to building Bible character we can escape our enemy and become more like our Master.

Youthful Lusts

The Lord knows those who are His, therefore, God's word says, "Let everyone who names the name of Christ depart from iniquity" (2 Tim. 2:19). Christians must cleanse themselves from sin in order to be ready for every good work of service in God's house, the church (2 Tim. 2:20-21). To help accomplish this, the young preacher Timothy was exhorted to "flee also youthful lusts; but pursue righteousness, faith, love, peace with those who call on the Lord out of a pure heart" (2 Tim. 2:22; 1 Tim. 6:11). This is sound advice for all young people.

Lust is defined as a strong desire or craving, and is used in 2 Timothy 2:22 of desires for things that are forbidden by God (see 1 John 2:15-17). Temptation to sin happens when we are enticed to fulfill a strong desire in a way that violates the will of God (Jas. 1:14). Sin actually happens when we give in to the enticements of lust and fulfill our desire by disobeying God (Jas. 1:15).

> By identifying the dangers and hindrances to building Bible character we can escape our enemy and become more like our Master.

So, we are urged to "not lust after evil things" like Israel did when they were in the wilderness (1 Cor. 10:6; Num. 11:4, 34). We must not yield to the cravings of sin.

There are some lusts that especially affect young people ("youthful lusts," 2 Tim. 2:22). As a young person you are experiencing a great deal of change in your life: your body is maturing, and so is your mind. You are choosing the direction you will take in life through education, job training, and similar life decisions. You are beginning to form associations and relations with others that will last a lifetime, including the selection of a mate in marriage. Above all, you should be choosing to be a faithful Christian now and for the rest of your life (Matt. 6:33; 16:24-26; Rom. 12:1-2). It is a mistake for the sinner to put off becoming a Christian. It is a mistake to delay developing godly character. In all of the new experiences of life you will be called on to make a choice: whether to be pure and faithful to Jesus or be defiled by fulfilling youthful lusts.

Flee Youthful Lusts

One of the best ways for young people to avoid sin and build godly character based on moral purity and faithfulness to Christ is to *flee*

> One of the best ways for young people to avoid sin and build godly character based on moral purity and faithfulness to Christ is to flee youthful lusts (2 Tim. 2:22). Do not put yourself into situations that increase temptation and make it easier to fulfill sinful lust.

youthful lusts (2 Tim. 2:22). Do not put yourself into situations that increase temptation and make it easier to fulfill sinful lust. For an example, consider how the teenager Joseph fled from his master's wife when she tried to entice him to sin (Gen. 39:6-13). Consider some of the things you can say and do to flee youthful lusts.

1. Flee youthful lusts by saying "no" to those who entice you. The power of peer pressure can be tremendous, either for good or for evil. It will help you say "no" when your friends or others tempt you to join them in sinning by deciding now what your answer will be before they entice you.

> My son, if sinners entice you, do not consent. If they say, "Come with us, Let us lie in wait to shed blood; Let us lurk secretly for the innocent without cause; Let us swallow them alive like Sheol, and whole, like those who go down to the Pit; we shall find all kinds of precious possessions, we shall fill our houses with spoil; cast in your lot among us, let us all have one purse" (Prov. 1:10-14).

Like Joseph, decide that you will not sin against God, and when others try to get you to join them in sin, flee by saying "no"!

2. Flee youthful lusts by not walking with sinners. "My son, do not walk in the way with them, Keep your foot from their path; for their feet run to evil, and they make haste to shed blood" (Prov. 1:15-16). Do not experiment with sin. Like the young lady who wore a pure white dress into the coal mine only to find it soiled with black soot when she exited, you cannot get as close to sin as possible without its influence hurting you. The devil's lie is "nothing is wrong with one drink," "one cigarette won't hurt," and "everybody has sex before marriage." Do not believe these lies; do not walk with sinners into evil: flee!

3. Flee youthful lusts by choosing your friends wisely. Friends have a tremendous influence on each one of us. So, it is very important to carefully choose who we put our trust in and whose advice we will follow. "Be not deceived: evil companionships corrupt good morals" (1 Cor. 15:33, ASV).

4. Flee youthful lusts by not making room for it in your life. Do not accommodate sin. Do not put yourself into situations that make it easy to sin: do not go to the dance; do not go to the bar; do not go to the public swimming pool or any place where sin's enticements are easily fulfilled. "But put on the Lord Jesus Christ, and make no provision for the flesh, to fulfill its lusts" (Rom. 13:14). Instead of compromising with sin we must refuse sin and put it to death in our lives (Col. 3:5-7; Rom. 6:4-14).

5. Flee youthful lusts by putting God's word in your heart. You can learn God's word and allow it to produce faith in your life. In God's word you will find protection against sin:

> How can a young man cleanse his way? By taking heed according to your word. With my whole heart I have sought you; oh, let me not wander from your commandments! Your word I have hidden in my heart, that I might not sin against you! Blessed are you, O Lord! Teach me your statutes (Psa. 119:9-12).

6. Flee youthful lusts by being an example of what is right. "Let no one despise your youth, but be an example to the believers in word, in conduct, in love, in spirit, in faith, in purity" (1 Tim. 4:12). You can be the person who leads others into right thinking and conduct. You do not have to follow others into sin. You can help others to godliness by setting an example of purity for them to follow.

7. Flee youthful lusts by daring to be different. Most young people are choosing to satisfy fleshly lusts. They are choosing a life of sin instead of righteousness. Christ challenges you to be different: to "walk in the Spirit" and "as sojourners and pilgrims" to "abstain from fleshly lusts which war against the soul" (Gal. 5:16;

1 Pet. 2:11). Live honorably before others: dare to be different from the world (1 Pet. 2:12)!

Things that can Hinder Young People from Fleeing Youthful Lusts

There are things about youth that can hinder the young person from fleeing lust and sin. By being aware of these hindrances you will be better equipped to flee sin and do what is right in God's sight.

1. The pride of youth. The pride of youth leads many young people to think they know better than their parents, better than grown-ups, and better than God about what is best for them. They think that they will live forever—or at least, that they will have plenty of time later to think about doing the will of God. That is not always the case. The wise man Solomon wrote, "Therefore remove sorrow from your heart, and put away evil from your flesh, for childhood and youth are vanity" (Eccl. 11:10). Youth does not last, and often with the passing of time one gets more and more set in his ways. Now is the time to flee sin and remember God (Eccl. 12:1; 2 Cor. 6:2). The wise young person understands that life is brief and uncertain and will build his character by fleeing sin.

2. The beauty and strength of youth. Some young people refuse to learn from the wisdom and experiences of their parents and others who love and care for them. The vitality and energy of youth leads some youth to think they are invincible (cf. Eccl. 9:11). But sin brings down the strongest of men (cf. Samson, Judg. 16:16-21). Bodily strength has its place and blessing, but strength of character endures long after muscles weaken and the body becomes frail (1 Tim. 4:8; Eccl. 12:1-7). The strength of youth alone will not prevent you from sinning.

3. The inexperience of youth. Unfortunately, some young people think they "know it all" and will not listen to the counsel and advice of older, wiser people like parents, grandparents, teachers, and fellow Christians. By refusing to heed the warnings against sin and its dangers, this young person is easy prey for Satan (1 Pet. 5:8). Learn to listen to the wise guidance and recommendations of older people who have the insight that comes with experience (cf. 1 Kings 12:1-19).

4. Low expectations. Sometimes young people do not expect moral character and faith out of themselves because adults do not expect it from them. Some adults despise (think little of) young people by expecting them to live carelessly and sinfully. If adults expect young people to "sow their wild oats" rest assured, they will! Young people can serve God; they do not have to sin. Expect to succeed by fleeing sin. Demand moral excellence of yourself and build your character through faith in Christ (Gal. 2:20).

> "Let no one despise your youth, but be an example to the believers in word, in conduct, in love, in spirit, in faith, in purity" (1 Tim. 4:12). You can be the person who leads others into right thinking and conduct.

5. Neglect. Like older people, young people can simply neglect doing what is right. There are many things that call for the time and attention of youth: school, jobs, recreation, etc. But to neglect the will of God causes you to be susceptible to sin and unable to build your character into the image of Christ. Jesus warned against neglecting the word of God:

> Now these are the ones sown among thorns; they are the ones who hear the word, and the cares of this world, the deceitfulness of riches, and the desires for other things entering in choke the word, and it becomes unfruitful (Mark 4:18-19).

Conclusion

The choices you make when you are young will shape and mold you into the person you will be when you are an adult. To live by faith you must "flee youthful lusts." By doing so you will be in a position to build your character with attributes of godliness. In the following lessons we will learn to "pursue righteousness, faith, love, peace with those who call on the Lord out of a pure heart" (2 Tim. 2:22).

Questions

True or False

_____ 1. There will come a time when the Christian can no longer build his or her character.

_____ 2. The apostle Paul pressed toward the goal of being more like Christ.

_____ 3. Lust means having little or no desire.

_____ 4. Israel lusted after evil things.

_____ 5. Young people are commanded by God to flee youthful lusts.

_____ 6. Joseph did not run from sin's temptation.

_____ 7. It is always easy to say "no" to sin.

_____ 8. Knowing God's word will not help keep you from sinning.

_____ 9. A young person can be an example to other Christians.

_____ 10. Young people always know what is best for them.

Questions for Discussion

1. Define "lust" as it is used in 2 Timothy 2:22. _____
   _____
   _____

2. What does Colossians 3:5 say we should do to evil desire? _____
   _____
   _____

3. Name some "youthful" lusts. _____
   _____

Are youthful lusts an excuse for sin or an explanation of sin (2 Tim. 2:22)? _____

4. Discuss why it could have been easy for Joseph to sin and also why he resisted its temptation (Gen. 39:1-13). _____
   _____
   _____

5. Why is it wise to not "walk in the way" with sinners (Prov. 1:15-16)? _____
   _____
   _____
   _____

6. How do friends influence your decisions? _____
   _____

   What kind of friends should you choose (1 Cor. 15:33)? _____
   _____
   _____

7. How much room should we make for sin in our lives? _____
   Discuss how this can happen (Rom. 13:11-14). _____
   _____

8. Why are young people sometimes tempted to think they have all the time in the world (Eccl. 11:10)? _____
   _____
   _____

9. Do you expect to sin or to flee sin?_____
   _____
   _____

10. Name some things that happen when we neglect the will of God (Mark 4:18-19; Heb. 6:9-12). __
    _____
    _____

Lesson 5

Pursue Righteousness

> In the gospel of Christ, God reveals how he saves sinners and pronounces them righteous (upright or just) in his sight (Rom. 1:16-17). When a sinner believes and obeys the gospel of Christ, his faith is accounted for righteousness (Rom. 4:5).

Introduction

After warning Timothy to flee youthful lusts, the apostle Paul directed his attention to things Timothy should vigorously pursue: "Flee also youthful lusts; but pursue righteousness, faith, love, peace with those who call on the Lord out of a pure heart" (2 Tim. 2:22; see also 1 Tim. 6:11).

To be faithful to Christ one must not only flee sin, but also pursue ("to run swiftly in order to catch some person or thing, to run after," *Thayer*) good things. There is no better time to start pursuing righteousness than when you are young (Eccl. 12:1).

What Is Righteousness?

The Bible says a great deal about righteousness. Broadly stated, righteousness describes "the state of him who is such as he ought to be ... the condition acceptable to God" (*Thayer*). Righteousness is "the character or quality of being right or just" and was formerly spelled "rightwiseness" (*Vine*). In Acts 10:34-35 we are assured that God accepts all who fear him and work righteousness.

In the strict sense of sinlessness, the Bible says "there is none righteous, no not one" (Rom. 3:10). This statement affirms that "all have sinned" (Rom. 3:23). But, when Paul urged Timothy to pursue righteousness he was not telling him to run after something that could not be attained. In the gospel of Christ, God reveals how he saves sinners and pronounces them righteous (upright or just) in his sight (Rom. 1:16-17). When a sinner believes and obeys the gospel of Christ, his faith is accounted for righteousness (Rom. 4:5).

The Bible describes people as righteous, not because they never sin, but because they trust God and obey his word. For instance, the parents of John (Zacharias and Elizabeth) were "both righteous before God, walking in all the commandments and ordinances of the Lord blameless" (Luke 1:6). Righteous people live by faith, like Abel, who "by faith offered to God a more excellent sacrifice than Cain, through which he obtained witness that he was righteous, God testifying of his gifts" (Heb. 11:4).

A righteous person is one whose way of thinking, feeling, and acting is completely conformed to the will of God. The righteous person respects the revealed word of God as the only valid standard of righteousness: "The judgments of God are true and righteous altogether"; and, "my tongue shall speak of your word, for all your commandments are righteousness" (Ps. 19:9; 119:172). The inspired word of God provides "instruction in righteousness" as it convicts the world of sin and righteousness (2 Tim. 3:16; John 16:8, 13).

The righteous person lives by faith with an upright heart because he is "filled with the fruits of righteousness" (Phil. 1:11). The righteous person treats others with honesty, justice, and fairness. Honor, duty, devotion, and piety are among the fruits of righteousness. (Thayer also defines righteousness as "integrity, virtue, purity of life, uprightness, correctness of thinking, feeling and acting.") The righteous person is blameless and innocent in his dealings with others. He treats others the way he wants to be treated and shows integrity in all things (Matt. 7:12; Prov. 24:29).

Pursuing Righteousness

When one becomes a Christian he must put off the old man of sin and "put on the new man which was created according to God, in true righteousness and holiness" (Eph. 4:24). True righteousness does not continue to live in sin; it puts away sin and serves the will of God (Eph. 4:17-24).

Jesus said, "But seek first the kingdom of God and His righteousness, and all these things shall be added to you" (Matt. 6:33). The Christian's priority in life must be to acknowledge and submit to the rule of God by doing those things that please God. The Christian pursues righteousness by becoming a bondservant or slave of righteousness. He does what is righteous in the sight of God. One cannot serve self or sin and be a servant of righteousness.

Just as food and water are necessary for physical life, spiritual food is essential for spiritual life. The food that sustains spiritual life is the word of God: "Man shall not live by bread alone, but by every word that proceeds from the mouth of God" (Matt. 4:4). Jesus said, "Do not labor for the food which perishes, but for the food which endures to everlasting life, which the Son of Man will give you" (John 6:27). Without proper spiritual nutrition from God's word, the Christian becomes weak in faith and fails to mature in the service of God.

Jesus assures us that, if we hunger and thirst after righteousness, we will be filled: "Blessed are those who hunger and thirst for righteousness, for they shall be filled" (Matt. 5:6). Here, Jesus challenges our desire for righteousness. Is your desire for righteousness so distinct and real that you crave it the way a hungry man craves food or a thirsty man craves water? As one commentator wrote, "Are you so intensely and sharply pained by your need for true righteousness that you would die unless you get it? Just how badly do you want to be righteous?" (*Gospel of Matthew*, Fowler, I: 215).

To pursue righteousness one must have a constant longing for it. (In Matthew 5:6 Jesus used the present participles "hungering" and "thirsting" to describe the continuous nature of desiring righteousness.) To hunger and thirst after righteousness one must have:

1. The priority of spiritual things. Righteousness is of primary importance to the meek person who, in poorness of spirit, mourns his sin (Matt. 5:3-5).

2. A preoccupation with doing the will of God. "As newborn babes, desire the pure milk of the word, that you may grow thereby" (1 Pet. 2:2). Just as a baby instinctively searches for its mother's milk, Christians long for God's word. Just as mother's milk sustains the life of a newborn child, the milk of God's word sustains our life in Christ. Just as milk helps a newborn child grow, the word of God helps us grow in righteous, godly living.

3. A strong desire to be right with God. "As the deer pants for the water brooks, so pants my soul for You, O God. My soul thirsts for God, for the living God. When shall I come and appear before God" (Psa. 42:1-2; cf. 63:1-6)? The one who pursues righteousness has an overriding desire to be right before God. He devotes himself to living righteously before God and man. Just as the desire for food prompts the hungry man to search for something to eat, one's longing to be upright before God compels him to pursue what God says is right (cf. Phil. 3:7-11).

Righteous Living

1. Righteousness involves a way of life. Having been saved by God's grace, the Christian is urged to living righteously. Jesus bore our sins on the cross so that we may die to sin and "live for righteousness" (1 Pet. 2:24). This is impressed upon us when Paul wrote, "For the grace of God that brings salvation has appeared to all men, teaching us that, denying ungodliness and worldly lusts, we should live soberly, righteously, and godly in the present age" (Tit. 2:11-12).

2. We cannot practice unrighteousness and stand in the grace of God. Holy living is coupled with "true righteousness" to describe the new man in Christ (Eph. 4:24). Children of light bear the fruit of the Spirit (that includes righteousness) and is acceptable to the Lord (Eph. 5:8-10). Since the kingdom of God consists of righteousness, one cannot live in unrighteousness and be a faithful member of the Lord's church (Rom. 14:17).

The epistle of 1 John discusses and encourages the habit of righteous living. There, we learn that "everyone who practices righteousness is born" of God (1 John 2:29). John warns us not to be deceived and misunderstand who is righteous: "Little children, let no one deceive you. He who practices righteousness is righteous, just as He is righteous" (1 John 3:7). If we do not "practice righteousness" we are "not of God" (1 John 3:10). One particular act of righteousness God expects of us is to "love one another" (1 John 3:11-15).

3. Practicing righteousness protects us from sin. We must "awake" out of spiritual slumber and put on the "breastplate of righteousness" in order to be protected from sin (1 Cor. 15:34; Eph. 6:14). By arming ourselves with righteous thinking and conduct we show ourselves to be servants of God (2 Cor. 6:7).

> In everything we do we must present our bodies to God as instruments (weapons) of righteousness (Rom. 6:13). By doing so, divine grace will reign over us rather than sin (Rom. 6:12, 14).

In everything we do we must present our bodies to God as instruments (weapons) of righteousness (Rom. 6:13). By doing so, divine grace will reign over us rather than sin (Rom. 6:12, 14).

4. In practicing righteous living we must avoid hypocrisy (pretending to be what we are not) and self-righteousness. Jesus rebuked the scribes and Pharisees because they pretended to be righteous when others were watching them, but their hearts were filled with corruption (Matt. 23:28; Luke 20:20). This is one reason why our righteousness must "exceed the righteousness of the scribes and Pharisees" or we will not enter the kingdom of heaven (Matt. 5:20). The self-righteous person trusts in himself; but the righteous person trusts in God (Luke 18:9-14).

The Trials of Righteousness

Not everyone will appreciate your decision to pursue righteousness. The light of truth and the righteous living it produces exposes the darkness of sin (John 3:19-21). Some would rather harm and hinder those who pursue righteousness than turn from their own sin. You must be prepared for the trials that come on those who hunger and thirst after righteousness.

Like the Lord, his disciples will be mistreated by unfaithful, unrighteous people (John 15:18-20). Yes, there is a price to be paid in order to be a disciple of Christ (Luke 14:25-33). That price may be that others will consider you to be strange and speak evil of you (1 Pet. 4:3-

> **Many blessings come from pursuing righteousness, including these:**
>
> - Spiritual fulfillment (Matt. 5:6).
> - Promise that our material needs will be met (Matt. 6:33; Psa. 37:25).
> - Salvation from sin (Acts 10:35; 1 Pet. 4:18).
> - The Lord sees, hears and delivers the righteous (Psa. 1:6; 34:15-22; 1 Pet. 3:10-12).
> - God favors, guards ,and is with the righteous (Psa. 5:12; 14:5).
> - The love of God (Psa. 11:7; 33:4-5; 146:8).
> - Rewarded by God (Psa. 18:20-24; 2 Tim. 4:8).
> - Boldness (Prov. 28:1).
> - Joy and rejoicing (Psa. 32:11; 33:1; 68:3).

4). They may make fun of you or in some other way try to get you to compromise your faith. Always remember to fear God rather than men (Matt. 10:28). What Peter said continues to be true:

> And who is he who will harm you if you become followers of what is good? But even if you should suffer for righteousness' sake, you are blessed. And do not be afraid of their threats, nor be troubled.... For it is better, if it is the will of God, to suffer for doing good than for doing evil (1 Pet. 3:13-14, 17).

When you face trouble because of righteous living, put your faith in the strength of the Lord to save you as He has promised (Psa. 37:39-40). "Cast your burden on the Lord, and he shall sustain you; He shall never permit the righteous to be moved" (Psa. 55:22).

The Blessings of Righteousness

Jesus assures those who pursue righteousness of divine blessings: "Blessed are those who are persecuted for righteousness' sake, for theirs is the kingdom of heaven. Blessed are you when they revile and persecute you, and say all kinds of evil against you falsely for my sake. Rejoice and be exceedingly glad, for great is your reward in heaven, for so they persecuted the prophets who were before you" (Matt. 5:10-12). Truly, "blessed are those who keep justice, and he who does righteousness at all times" (Psa. 106:3).

Conclusion

Unrighteousness hinders the progress of the truth of God and exposes the unrighteous person to divine wrath (Rom. 1:18). But, "He who follows righteousness and mercy finds life, righteousness and honor" (Prov. 21:21).

God will judge the righteous and the wicked (Eccl. 3:17). When Jesus returns he will judge the world in righteousness (Acts 17:31). If you will pursue righteousness now and for the rest of your life, when Jesus appears you will receive the victory crown of the righteous (2 Tim. 4:7-8).

"The wicked man does deceptive work, but he who sows righteousness will have a sure reward. As righteousness leads to life, so he who pursues evil pursues it to his own death" (Prov. 11:18-19).

NOTES

Questions

True or False

____ 1. Nobody can be righteous today.

____ 2. All it takes to be righteous is to flee sin.

____ 3. God's means of bringing sinners to righteousness is revealed in the gospel.

____ 4. The righteous person is honest in all his dealings with others.

____ 5. Those who live by faith will seek the righteousness of God before the material things of life.

____ 6. Those who hunger and thirst after righteousness are sad because they are hungry.

____ 7. Christians are bondservants of righteousness.

____ 8. Everybody will like you if you pursue righteousness.

____ 9. The Lord leads his people in the paths of righteousness.

____ 10. The righteous will receive a crown of righteousness.

Questions for Discussion

1. Define "the way of righteousness" as it is used in 2 Peter 2:20-21. _____

2. The scope and advantages of righteous living are discussed in Proverbs 10. From that passage, list the lifestyle of the righteous and the blessings that result. _____

3. What does the righteous person do according to Proverbs 11:30? _____

4. Does a righteous person speak lies (Prov. 12:17; 13:5)? _____

5. How does the righteous living of citizens have an impact on their nation (Prov. 14:34)? _____

6. Of what does the kingdom consist according to Romans 14:17? _____

7. What does the person find who follows righteousness and mercy (Prov. 21:21)? _____

8. According to 1 Peter 4:18, how are the righteous saved? _____
   What does this mean? _____

9. What kind of a preacher was Noah (2 Pet. 2:5)? _____

10. Discuss the character or nature of sin and righteousness using Revelation 22:11. _____

Lesson 6

Pursue Faith

Kinds of Faith

- Weak, Rom. 4:19
- Little, Matt. 6:30
- Profitless, Jas. 2:14
- Dead, Jas. 2:17, 20
- Like demons, Jas. 2:19
- Great, Matt. 8:10
- Hidden, John 9:42
- Visible, Matt. 9:2
- Saving, Luke 7:50; Heb. 10:39
- Full of, Acts 6:5, 8
- Steadfast, Col. 2:5
- Working, 1 Thess. 1:3; Jas. 2:20
- Growing, 2 Thess. 1:3
- Sincere, 1 Tim. 1:5
- Genuine, 2 Tim. 1:5; 1 Pet. 1:7
- Sound, Titus 2:2
- Rich, Jas. 2:5
- Mature, Jas. 2:22
- Precious, 2 Pet. 1:1
- Holy, Jude 20

Introduction

God wants young people to pursue faith (2 Tim. 2:22; 1 Tim. 6:11). Maybe you think faith is only for your parents, grandparents, and older people. But, the Bible is full of examples of young people who chose to live by faith and did great things in the service of God. You can, too.

What Is Faith?

Faith is often misunderstood. Faith is not a blind leap in the dark. It is not wishful thinking. Faith is not defined as an emotional feeling you have toward something or someone. Furthermore, being "faithful" to God means much more than just being present at the Bible classes and worship services of a local church of Christ.

Faith is defined in Hebrews 11:1 as "the substance of things hoped for, the evidence of things not seen." Faith is belief; a conviction, an assurance, a firm persuasion and a confident trust that rests upon trustworthy evidence or testimony. Faith, in turn, gives substance to one's hope (cf. Rom. 5:1-2). But, without faith it is impossible to please God (Heb. 11:6). We cannot hope to please God and go to heaven if we do not put our faith in Him.

Faith is produced by accepting the evidence and testimony contained in the word of God: "So then faith comes by hearing, and hearing by the word of God" (Rom. 10:17). For instance, the apostle John wrote about the miracles of Jesus so "that you may believe that Jesus is the Christ, the Son of God, and that believing you may have life in His name" (John 20:30-31). The only way we can be sure that we have the right kind of faith is to find evidence for it in the word of God. The Bereans are commended for searching the Scriptures to see if what they were being taught was truly the word and will of God. When they discovered it was, they believed (Acts 17:11-12).

1. You need faith in the true and living God (Heb. 11:6; Acts 17:22-31; 1 Cor. 8:4-6; Eph. 4:6). There are many false gods in this world: the gods of pleasure, popularity, materialism, greed, sensuality, etc. Men still make for themselves gods that they serve, but there is only one God, the God who created us, sustains us and saves us in His Son Jesus Christ.

2. You need faith that the Bible is the inspired word of God (2 Tim. 3:16-17; 2 Pet. 1:20-21; Gal. 1:11-12). The Bible is not the product of human wisdom and knowledge. Throughout time men have unsuccessfully tried to discredit the Bible as the work of men and not God. But, God's word "endures forever." God continues to expect us to believe and obey His word (1 Pet. 1:22-25).

3. You need faith that Jesus is the Son of God. The Bible records the words and mighty works of Jesus in order to convince us that He is the Christ (John 20:30-31; 5:36-39, 46-47; 14:11). Unless we believe Jesus is the Son of God we will be lost in our sins (John 8:23-24).

4. You need faith to become a child of God. Believers in Christ are not automatically saved from their sins. "But as many as received Him, to them He gave the right to become children of God, to those who believe in His name" (John 1:12). Only those who believe in Jesus through the gospel will be saved (Rom. 1:16-17).

Living by Faith

To live by faith one must hear and obey the word of God (Rom. 10:17). Jesus said the wise person hears His word and does it (Matt. 7:24-27). This begins by becoming a Christian (Mark 16:15-16; Acts 2:36-41, 47; 16:30-34). It is not enough just to believe in God, because "even the demons believe—and tremble" (Jas. 2:19). A person who truly believes God will obey the word of God (Matt. 7:21-23).

It has been said that "faith is taking God at His word and doing whatever He says." The Bible supports this view of faith. It is not enough to mentally agree with what the Bible says. Unless we are *doing* what the Bible says we are not living by faith.

> But without faith it is impossible to please Him, for he who comes to God must believe that He is, and that He is a rewarder of those who diligently seek Him (Heb. 11:6).

For we walk by faith, not by sight. We are confident, yes, well pleased rather to be absent from the body and to be present with the Lord. Therefore we make it our aim, whether present or absent, to be well pleasing to Him. For we must all appear before the judgment seat of Christ, that each one may receive the things done in the body, according to what he has done, whether good or bad (2 Cor. 5:7-10).

When the following three steps are combined they constitute walking by faith:

1. Hear the word of God (1 Sam. 3:10; Rom. 10:17). It is important to listen carefully to what the Bible says (Luke 8:8, 18). We listen to the word of God by reading the Scriptures and by hearing it taught. By carefully listening to the words of Christ we can understand His will for us: "Why do you not understand my speech? Because you are not able to listen to my word" (John 8:43). "He who is of God hears God's words" (John 8:47).

2. Believe the word of God. The man in Acts 8:35-37 is an example of one who heard the word of God and believed it. We must trust that God's word is right and that he has the power to do what he says.

3. Obey the word of God (Matt. 4:4; Jas. 1:21-22). Jesus asked, "But why do you call me 'Lord, Lord,' and not do the things which I say?" (Luke 6:46). Walking by faith means to live every day of our life trusting and obeying God in all things (Gal. 2:20).

Hebrews 11 gives many examples of people who walked by faith. In every case, the faith that pleases God is shown to be an active, obedient faith. God expects young people to walk by faith, too.

Pursue Faith

When Paul told Timothy to "pursue ... faith" he was speaking to someone who already had "genuine faith" (2 Tim. 1:5). Christians should progress in their faith (Phil. 1:25), abound in faith (2 Cor. 8:7), grow exceedingly in faith (2 Thess. 1:3), and be rich in faith (Jas. 2:5). No limit is placed on the increase of personal faith in God.

Pursuing faith requires personal commitment. When the apostles asked Jesus to increase their faith, he taught them a lesson on being faithful servants (Luke 17:5-10). We must commit ourselves to serving the will of Jesus instead of ourselves. When we do so, our faith will grow. This commitment to grow in faith is reflected in 2 Peter 1:5-11, where the Christian is commanded to diligently strengthen his faith through spiritual growth. If we fail to grow in our faith we are in danger of developing an "evil heart of unbelief in departing from the living God" (Heb. 3:12).

Faith and Character

Pursuing faith is a deliberate choice to trust God and do His will. Faith reflects your character as well as reinforces it. Without genuine faith in Christ the character we should develop will always be incomplete. As examples, faith is needed to develop and keep the following character traits:

1. Honesty. There are certainly honest people who are not Christians. Still, the Bible not only defines honesty, it also teaches us its value and enduring qualities (Prov. 10:9; 11:3; 12:19; 19:1). The Christian chooses honesty because of his faith in God (Eph. 4:25-32).

2. Moral purity. The moral purity of the Christian is defined by what the Bible says is pure, not what your friends, the media, and present society says is moral (Matt. 5:8; 1 John 2:15-17; Phil. 4:8; 1 Tim. 1:5). Godly character requires faith in the moral standard of God's word.

3. Choosing friends. Our character is affected by the friends we choose: "Do not be deceived: 'Evil company corrupts good habits'" (1 Cor. 15:33). Your faith in God is revealed as you select your friends.

> **The Lord expects young Christians to worship in spirit and in truth like all other Christians (John 4:24). He expects you to serve Christ with the abilities and opportunities he gives you (Matt. 25:14-17; Rom. 12:3-8).**

4. Hard work. One of the best ways to see the character of a person is to watch how he works. Are they diligent at all times, or only when the boss is watching (Eph. 6:5-8)? You show your faith when you understand that the attitude you have toward your employer reflects your attitude toward God (Col. 3:22-24).

5. Faithfulness to Christ. The Lord expects young Christians to worship in spirit and in truth like all other Christians (John 4:24). He expects you to serve Christ with the abilities and opportunities he gives you (Matt. 25:14-17; Rom. 12:3-8). He expects you to understand His will and live in harmony with it (Eph. 5:15-17). When you faithfully serve Christ you reveal that your character is built upon faith (Luke 17:5-10).

Trials of Faith

The character of faith is revealed when your faith is put to the test. Your adversary the devil is stalking you, looking for an opportunity to turn you from faith to unbelief (1 Pet. 5:8). He can be withstood when you allow the gospel ("the faith") to direct your life of faith (1 Pet. 5:9).

NOTES

> By faith, Moses chose to suffer for doing the will of God instead of sinning against God, because he valued the will of God more than the riches of this world (Heb. 11:24-26). When you resist temptation you reveal your faith and your character, and you please God.

Faith is powerful. The power of faith does not come from the person who is living by faith, but from God in whom a person puts his faith. By the power of faith, the walls of Jericho fell when Israel obeyed God (Heb. 11:30). David killed the giant Goliath, not because he was stronger, but because of his faith—he trusted God would give him the victory (1 Sam. 17:37-50). Through faith, men "subdued kingdoms, worked righteousness, obtained promises, stopped the mouths of lions, quenched the violence of fire, escaped the edge of the sword, out of weakness were made strong, became valiant in battle, turned to flight the armies of the aliens" (Heb. 11:33-34). We must never forget that it is through the power of faith in Jesus Christ that God saves sinners by his grace (John 3:16; 8:24; Rom. 1:16; Eph. 2:8-9).

Faith will be tried (Acts 14:22; Jas. 1:2-4; 1 Pet. 1:6-9). Faith is tried by the temptation to do what God forbids as well as the temptation to not do what God wants (Jas. 1:12-16; 4:17). Joseph refused to sin against God when his faith was put to the test (Gen. 39:6-9). By faith, Moses chose to suffer for doing the will of God instead of sinning against God, because he valued the will of God more than the riches of this world (Heb. 11:24-26). When you resist temptation you reveal your faith and your character, and you please God.

Faith is rewarded. "For whatever is born of God overcomes the world. And this is the victory that has overcome the world—our faith" (1 John 5:4). Unbelief will never please God (Heb. 11:6). This is why Christians must continue to grow in Christ and be faithful in all things. If Christians fall into faithlessness they will be lost (Heb. 3:12-14; 4:11).

Conclusion

Young people can live by faith. To do so, listen to and learn the word of God; trust that it is right in all things; and obey Jesus in everything. By pursuing this kind of simple faith your character will become more and more like Christ.

Questions

True or False

_____ 1. Young people cannot live by faith because they do not understand the Bible.

_____ 2. God wants young people to be an example of faith.

_____ 3. Faith is blind and must be different for every person.

_____ 4. Faith without works is dead.

_____ 5. John wrote about the miracles of Jesus so people would believe and have life.

_____ 6. Living by faith means believing there is one God.

_____ 7. You can be saved and go to heaven if you do not believe Jesus is the Son of God.

_____ 8. Faith is defined as being sincere about the things of God.

Questions for Discussion

1. What is faith? _____

   How important is faith (Heb. 11:1, 6)? _____

   _____

2. What are some common misunderstandings of faith? _____

   _____

   _____

3. According to Hebrews 11:1, what does faith support? _____

   _____

   _____

4. Can a person who does not believe the Bible is the word of God have true faith in God? _____

   Why or why not? _____

   _____

5. What do believers have the power to do (John 1:12)? _____

   _____

6. What does it mean to walk by faith? _____

   _____

7. Name and explain the three steps that make up walking by faith. _____

   _____

   _____

8. What does faith have to do with character? _____
   _____

9. Can people become faithless (lose their faith)? _____ Why does this happen? _____
   _____

   What is their spiritual condition (Heb. 4:12-14; 4:11; 6:4-6)? _____
   _____

10. Name three Old Testament characters from Hebrews 11 and tell about their faith: What did they do "by faith"? What were the results of their faith? _____
    _____
    _____

11. Name and discuss some things you must do "by faith" in order to be a faithful child of God. ____
    _____
    _____

12. Discuss how can you increase your faith (Luke 17:5-10; John 8:31-32; Rom. 10:17)? _____
    _____
    _____
    _____

Lesson 7

Pursue Love

Introduction

In the quest to build Bible character, no trait will be more worthy of your pursuit than love. "God is love," and he wants Christians to "walk in love" (1 John 4:8; Eph. 5:2). God expects you to pursue love while in your youth (1 Tim. 6:11; 2 Tim. 2:22).

In the 1960s the Beatles popularized the sentiment, "all you need is love" with one of their songs. Unfortunately, the phrase was used to encourage conduct that was not true love, but the fulfillment of selfish lust and self-defined "love." In truth, what many, many people mean by "love" is not what we "need" at all. What is truly needed is a scriptural understanding of love. A scriptural understanding of love will enable you to "love the Lord your God with all your heart, with all your soul, and with all your mind," and to love "your neighbor as yourself" (Matt. 22:37-39).

What Is love?

Humans have spent their history pondering that question. Countless poems have been penned, songs sung, and books written, both extolling its virtue and exploring its complexities. Unfortunately, people often do not accurately define love. The love we are interested in understanding and living by is revealed to us in the Bible.

The Greek language in which the New Testament was first written had several words for "love." This can present a problem to speakers of English, who use the one word "love" to describe a wide range of emotions, attitudes, and conduct. You may "love" chocolate, but not in the way you "love" your parents. And, while we are to "love" our enemies they do not receive from us the same affection shared between husbands and wives. You see, unless we understand the different kinds of love that are discussed in the New Testament we will be ill-equipped to pursue love in the right way.

1. Eros. This word, from which is derived the English word *erotic*, is not used in the New Testament. The Greeks used this word to describe the physical expressions of sensuality and sexuality between the sexes. This word came to be connected with lust rather than love by the time the New Testament was written.

> . . . unless we understand the different kinds of love that are discussed in the New Testament we will be ill-equipped to pursue love in the right way.

2. Storge. This word is not found in the New Testament, either. It was used in secular Greek as a word for family love.

3. Philos. This word represents the expression of warm, tender affection, of cherishing. Barclay noted that this word "describes a warm, intimate, tender relationship of body, mind and spirit" (*Flesh and Spirit*, 64). This word describes the kindness of loving one's fellow man (Acts 28:2); of the cherishing love of a wife toward her husband and a mother toward her children (Tit. 2:4); and of the brotherly love Christians should have for each other (Rom. 12:10; 1 Thess. 4:9-10; Heb. 13:1). Without question, we should be "lovers of God" (2 Tim. 3:4).

4. Agape. This love has been defined as "unconquerable benevolence" and "undefeatable goodwill" (Barclay, 65). It always seeks the highest good of its object. It is not affected by the way others treat it: it continues to act in the best interests of others.

While the world defines love on a purely physical plane (emotional, physical, erotic,

> **Love is . . .**
> **(1 Cor. 13:4-8)**
>
> - Longsuffering
> - Kind
> - Does not envy
> - Does not brag
> - Is not puffed up
> - Is not rude
> - Is not selfish
> - Is not provoked
> - Thinks no evil
> - Does not rejoice in iniquity
> - Rejoices in the truth
> - Bears all things
> - Believes all things
> - Hopes all things
> - Endures all things
> - Love never fails

etc.), the Bible elevates love to the essential motive of life (1 Cor. 13:1-3). This love is an act of one's will. For instance, one does not love his enemy with warm affection (*philos*), but Christ says we must love (*agapao*) our enemy by doing him good (Matt. 5:44). Regardless of how others treat us, we are to show *agape* toward them.

This love is the active expression of goodwill—the very essence and expression of God and of knowing God (1 John 4:7-10). God has shown us His love to all of us in the death of Jesus for our sins (Rom. 5:8). God's love for us is the compelling reason for us to love Him and to love one another (1 John 4:11). "We love Him because He first loved us" (1 John 4:19).

A thorough discussion of love is found in 1 Corinthians 13:

1. The motive of love (1 Cor. 13:1-3). Love is the supreme motive for all we say and do. It is one thing to say we love someone or something, but something else to show love by our actions toward others (1 John 3:16-18). 1 Corinthians 13:1-3 teaches us that, even if our actions are good, if they are not motivated by love, they are worthless before God.

2. The character of love (1 Cor. 13:4-7). In this passage we see the goodwill of love that is always directed toward others.

3. The permanence of love (1 Cor. 13:8-13). The inspired apostle was teaching of a time when miraculous spiritual gifts (1 Cor. 12) would cease among the people of God. But, love is always needed. Love continues on, strengthening faith and hope. Love is the greatest: Without love, faith has no approved motive (see 1 Cor. 13:1-3); without love, hope becomes selfish and disappointing (see 1 Cor. 13:4-7; Rom. 5:5).

Remember, the world confuses love and lust. It defines love on the basis of outward beauty and physical attraction. The world tells young people that satisfying the lusts of the flesh and of the eyes is love (1 John 2:15-16). It does not know the love of God.

Responsibilities of Love

We often think of love as something we want from others. And it is true that God expects others to love us. But, even when others do not love us the way they should, God expects us to love them (Matt. 7:12). Love is not selfish nor does it keep a running account of how others have offended it (1 Cor. 13:5).

We have the responsibility to love:

1. God. We must fully and completely love God (Mark 12:30). Love for God is shown by humbly obeying his commands without complaint (John 14:15; 1 John 5:3).

2. Our neighbor as ourselves (Mark 12:31). The Samaritan who cared for the injured man was moved by love for a stranger, and teaches us how to be a neighbor to others (Luke 10:29-37).

3. The brotherhood (1 Pet. 2:17). If we cannot love our brethren in Christ, whom we see and live around, how can we love God whom we have not seen (1 John 4:20)?

4. Our enemies (Matt. 5:43-48). To love those who mistreat us, or even hate us, is to love in the same way God loves. Not only does God show His love for all men in giving and sustaining life here on earth, He has shown His great love for sinners (enemies) by giving His Son to die so sinners can be saved (John 3:16; Rom. 5:6-8). We cannot expect God to be pleased with us if we do not love others they way He has loved us.

5. The word of God. "Oh how I love your law! It is my meditation all the day" (Ps.

119:97). When we love the word of God we will be careful to learn it and follow it always.

Practicing Love

Pursuing love takes a lot of effort! It is not easy to practice love. It requires consistently putting the interests and concerns of others before self. It demands devotion to God and His truth, a devotion that will do His will without grumbling and complaining.

Practicing love toward fellow Christians shows we are disciples of Jesus (John 13:34-35).

In addition to loving other Christians, young people have some particular areas where love should be practiced.

1. Toward family. God wants you to love your parents by honoring them with respect and obedience (Eph. 6:1-3). And, He wants you to love your siblings, too. There should not be strife between brothers and sisters (cf. Gen. 13:8).

2. Toward friends. Friendship is a wonderful blessing, offering companionship, encouragement and strength (Eccl. 4:9-12; Prov. 17:17). And, like any other relationship, friendship is built on trust and love. The selfish, unloving person will not have many friends. To have friends we must show the love of a friend to others (Prov. 18:24). Jesus did this by laying down His life for His friends (John 15:13). When we obey His commands, we are His friends (John 15:14).

3. Toward strangers. Sometimes we are tempted to disregard or give little thought to strangers. But God wants us to love strangers. The word translated "hospitality" is *philoxenos*, "loving strangers" (1 Pet. 4:9; cf. Heb. 13:2). Kindness and consideration that is shown to strangers does not go unnoticed.

4. When you date. Young people need to understand what real love is and remember what it is when they date. Since the world defines love as fulfilling lustful desires, it is imperative that real love be a part of your character. For instance, if *agape* is a part of your character, then you will not use or be deceived by such selfish lies as, "if you really love me you will have pre-marital sex with me." The person who truly loves you will not lure you into sin. And, with real love in your heart, you will not tempt your boyfriend or girlfriend to engage in any activity that is sinful in God's sight. The love that godly young people will pursue comes from a pure heart (2 Tim. 2:22).

The Rewards of Love

Love does not go out in search of recognition and reward. It is not serving itself, but God and others. But rest assured, God sees and

> Love does not go out in search of recognition and reward. It is not serving itself, but God and others. But rest assured, God sees and rewards those who walk in love.

1. Love grants victory over the trials and troubles of life (Rom. 8:35-39). The love of God does not shield us from having trouble; it protects us so that we can conquer whatever challenges confront our faith. As a young person, your faith will be tested. But, if you will always love and obey God you will not be overcome by evil.

2. Loving Jesus brings the salvation of your soul (1 Pet. 1:8-9). Even though you have not seen Jesus Christ, we are to love him. Loving Christ is the action of faith—obeying His word (John 14:15). When you obey Jesus from a heart of love you can be sure He will bless your faith with victory (1 John 5:3-4).

Conclusion

If we do not love others then we do not know God, because God is love (1 John 4:8). Everything we do should be done with love (1 Cor. 16:14). The Scriptures encourage us to "keep yourselves in the love of God" (Jude 21). And "this is love, that we walk according to His commandments" (2 John 8).

NOTES
___
___
___
___
___

Questions

True or False

_____ 1. God does not tell young people to pursue love.

_____ 2. Love is known by what it does (1 John 3:16-18).

_____ 3. The first commandment is to love God will all our heart, soul, mind, and strength.

_____ 4. *Philos* is the highest form of love.

_____ 5. *Agape* is the love God has shown sinners.

_____ 6. As long as you do what is right it doesn't matter why you do it.

_____ 7. Love means having no responsibilities to God or others.

_____ 8. Love will fail.

_____ 9. God says it is okay not to love some people.

_____ 10. Before you love someone you have to see him.

Questions for Discussion

1. What did Jesus say was the "first and great commandment"? _____

   What does this mean (Matt. 22:37-38)? _____

2. What does it mean that "all the Law and the Prophets" hang on the commands to love God and your neighbor (Matt.22:39-40)? _____

3. What four words were used in the Greek language for "love"? Which two are used in the NewTestament? _____

4. Define *philos*, and give two places in the New Testament where it is used. _____

5. Define *agape*, and give two places in the New Testament where it is used. _____

6. According to 1 John 4:7-11, (a) Why should we love one another? _____

   (b) Who is born of God and knows God? _____

(c) How did God show love to us? _____

_____

7. Discuss the difference between love and lust: How can you know the difference? _____

_____

Why does it matter that you recognize this difference? _____

_____

8. Name the traits of love given in 1 Corinthians 13:4-8. _____ \

_____

How will this kind of love improve the family? _____

_____

How will it improve the church? _____

_____

9. Name some people and things that we must love, and discuss how that is done. Give scriptures to support your conclusions. _____

_____

_____

10. Does a woman need to learn how to love her husband and children? _____ What about men (Tit. 2:4; Eph. 5:25-29; 1 Pet. 3:7)?_____

11. What kind of love should be looked for in the person you decide to marry? Why? _____

_____

_____

12. Why is obeying Jesus described as loving Him in John 14:15 and 2 John 8? _____

_____

_____

13. What is a "sweet-smelling aroma" to God in Ephesians 5:2?_____

_____

_____

14. What will tell others that you are a disciple of Jesus? Why? John 13:35 _____

_____

_____

Lesson 8

Pursue Peace

Different Kinds of Peace

- National tranquility, Acts 24:2; 1 Tim. 2:1-2
- Harmony between individuals, 1 Thess. 5:13
- Security, safety, prosperity and happiness, Jas. 2:16
- The way of salvation brought by the Messiah, Luke 1:78-79
- Peace with God (the contentment of a life of faith), Rom. 15:13
- The eternal comfort enjoyed by the righteous after the judgment, Rom. 2:10

Introduction

As you build Bible character you will find peace to be a tremendous blessing—and a tremendous challenge. Few things are sought after more in this world than peace; whether it is peace among nations, peace among neighbors, peace within families, peace among friends, or peace in the church. There is no question that the world is a better place where peace exists. Peace is a worthy pursuit (2 Tim. 2:22). And yet, peace eludes many who pursue it.

One reason peace is hard to attain and maintain is that it is greatly misunderstood. This leads to a false sense of peace. For example, the people of ancient Jerusalem wanted peace—they even thought they had peace—yet, they had no real and lasting peace because they were sinning against God (Jer. 6:13-15). Peace cannot rule where sin reigns.

What Is Peace?

Two things are necessary in order to have genuine peace. On the one hand, peace is the absence of conflict. When open hostility ceases between warring nations, men call it "peace." You probably know people who are not openly fighting each other, but who are not "at peace" with each other. For example, a person is not really at peace with his neighbor if he has resentment, ill will, and suspicion toward him in his heart. Open conflict may not be happening, but peace does not characterize the relationship. Real peace takes more than just not fighting with someone.

Genuine peace also involves the presence of tranquility, contentment, serenity, security, and safety. "The work of righteousness will be peace, and the effect of righteousness, quietness and assurance forever. My people will dwell in a peaceful habitation, in secure dwellings, and in quiet resting places" (Isa. 32:17-18). Peace is much more than a temporary cease fire between enemies. Peace exists when a relationship is defined by calm contentment rather than aggressive confrontation.

What Destroys Peace?

Sin destroys peace by introducing hostility and conflict into one's life. It is our sins that disrupt the peaceful harmony we have with God and with others (see Isa. 59:1-2; Col. 1:21; Jas. 4:1-2). Therefore, sin must be removed if we are to have actual peace with God and men.

Jesus Is Our Peace

God is "not the author of confusion, but of peace" (1 Cor. 14:33). Everything God does for us is so we can be at peace with him. God is the source of peace ("grace to you and peace from God our Father and the Lord Jesus Christ," Rom. 1:7; 2 Thess. 3:16) and the embodiment of peace; he is the "God of peace" (Heb. 13:20).

The Savior was prophesied as the "Prince of Peace" because He would establish peace between man and God by saving sinners (Isa. 9:6; Luke 2:14). You were an enemy of God

> Instead of allowing the world of sin to control your attitudes, your motives, and your conduct, the peace of God must "rule in your hearts."

before you were saved from your sins by Jesus Christ. When you obeyed the gospel you received peace with God. By His death on the cross, peace with God is now available to all sinners (Rom. 5:10). The first thing to do in pursuing peace is making sure that you are at peace with God through His Son, Jesus Christ.

Peace with God is obtained through the sacrifice of His Son Jesus Christ and our faith in Him: "Therefore, having been justified by faith, we have peace with God through our Lord Jesus Christ" (Rom. 5:1). The apostle confidently affirms that Jesus "is our peace" (Eph. 2:14).

A person must be at peace with God in order to have genuine peace with others. The Jews and Gentiles did not have peace between themselves until Christ brought peace to all men through His gospel:

> "For He Himself is our peace, who has made both one, and has broken down the middle wall of separation, having abolished in His flesh the enmity, that is, the law of commandments contained in ordinances, so as to create in Himself one new man from the two, thus making peace, and that He might reconcile them both to God in one body through the cross, thereby putting to death the enmity. And He came and preached peace to you who were afar off and to those who were near. For through Him we both have access by one Spirit to the Father" (Eph. 2:14-18).

Today, Jews and Gentiles have peace with God in one body, the church of Christ.

Peace is the goal and calling of the Christian's life. Now that you have peace with God through your forgiveness in Christ, you are called upon to be at peace with others: "If it is possible, as much as depends on you, live peaceably with all men" (Rom. 12:18); "Blessed are the peacemakers, for they shall be called sons of God" (Matt. 5:9). We cannot live in hatred, malice, and strife toward people and think that we are at peace with God.

Christians are called to peace by the gospel of Christ: "And let the peace of God rule in your hearts, to which also you were called in one body; and be thankful" (Col. 3:15). Instead of allowing the world of sin to control your attitudes, your motives, and your conduct, the peace of God must "rule in your hearts." Like an umpire who calls the balls and strikes, the peace of God is the standard to be followed in how we treat others. Jesus said to treat others the way we wish to be treated (Matt. 7:12). Surely, we wish others to treat us peacefully. We can do no less toward others if we are to be faithful to Christ.

What Is Necessary to Pursue Peace

1. The gospel of Christ. To pursue peace you must obey the gospel of peace (Rom. 10:15; Eph. 6:15). The gospel not only saves us from our past sins, it also shows us the way of life that keeps us at peace with God and with people.

2. A pure heart. A clean heart is essential as you build Bible character in your life. Paul told Timothy to pursue peace by joining with all those who "call on the Lord out of a pure heart" (2 Tim. 2:22). A heart that is defiled by sin (such as hate) cannot be at peace with God or with man.

3. Wisdom from above. Two kinds of wisdom exist in this world; earthly wisdom, and heavenly wisdom. James assures us that "the wisdom that is from above is first pure, then peaceable, gentle, willing to yield, full of mercy and good fruits, without partiality and without hypocrisy" (Jas. 3:17). Every description of heavenly wisdom reveals a commitment to peace with God and with men. It takes wisdom to know how to pursue peace in this life. God's word is the source of wisdom that gives you peace throughout life: "My son, do not forget my law, but let your heart keep my commands; for length of days and long life and peace they will add to you" (Prov. 3:1-2).

4. Unselfishness. Strife comes from selfish choices and selfish actions. One reason for "wars and fights" is the selfish treatment of others (Jas. 4:1-4). Pursuing and keeping peace requires self-sacrifice and considering others first before you think of yourself (Phil. 2:3-4).

5. Humility. Only by humbling ourselves before others are we able to pursue and keep peace. After rebuking the brethren for their "friendship with the world," James urged them to humble themselves in the sight of the Lord (Jas. 4:6-10). Pride stands in the way of peace; humility opens the door to it.

6. Kindness. Kindness in your heart will help you be a peaceful person. It takes determination and hard work to always show kindness. By being kind you will be like God and His kindness toward us in Christ. "Let all bitterness, wrath, anger, clamor, and evil speaking be put away from you, with all malice. And be kind to one another, tenderhearted, forgiving one another, even as God in Christ forgave you" (Eph. 4:31-32).

7. Pray for peace. Prayers for rulers are so that "we may live a quiet and peaceable life in all godliness and reverence" (1 Tim. 2:1-2). Praying for our enemies should include supplications for peace (Matt. 5:44). A peaceful person is a praying person who relies on God for his or her life of tranquility and safety.

8. Faith in God to right the wrongs of this life. Taking vengeance on someone who wrongs you prevents you from pursuing peace. "Repay no one evil for evil. Have regard for good things in the sight of all men. If it is possible, as much as depends on you, live peaceably with all men" (Rom. 12:17-18). It is up to us to "overcome evil with good" (Rom. 12:20-21). God has promised that He will fully judge and punish evildoers (Rom. 12:19).

Be at Peace

Building peacefulness into your character is not optional if you wish to please God; He commands you to do so. "Therefore let us pursue the things which make for peace and the things by which one may edify another" (Rom. 14:19). Consider some of the areas of life where you will need to pursue peace.

1. Peace with God. As noted previously, sin produces conflict between you and God (Isa. 59:1-2). If you are to have peace in your heart and soul you must be saved from your sins by the Prince of Peace. Jesus said to come to Him and He will give us rest (Matt. 11:28). The removal of sin removes the conflict and replaces it with the joy of harmony with God; this is true peace.

2. Peace with all people. Some people are not peaceful; they thrive on conflict and selfishly fighting with others. Jesus was put to death by such evil people. Still, He teaches us to follow His example and do not return "evil for evil or reviling for reviling, but on the contrary, blessing" (1 Pet. 3:9). As much as it is possible, the person who follows the example of Jesus will live peaceably with others (Rom. 12:8).

NOTES

> Jesus said, "Blessed are the peacemakers, for they shall be called sons of God" (Matt. 5:9). You are becoming more and more like God as you develop peacefulness as a part of your character.

3. Peace in your family. For families to flourish they must live in peace. In homes where peace prevails, blessings abound. Many souls are lost because peace at home was destroyed by abuse, conflict, and strife.

4. Among your friends. Friends are great blessings throughout life (Prov. 17:17). But, to have friends we must be a friend (Prov. 18:24). No one wants a friend who loves to argue and fight. Developing a peaceable character includes learning to forgive and forget so that friendship is strengthened and not destroyed when you are wronged.

5. In the church. A peaceful church is a great blessing from God. Peace amplifies our unity and enhances our possibilities of service. So, we must diligently guard it, maintaining it as our bond (Eph. 4:3).

Wonderful Blessings

Jesus said, "Blessed are the peacemakers, for they shall be called sons of God" (Matt. 5:9). You are becoming more and more like God as you develop peacefulness as a part of your character. What a wonderful blessing!

James wrote, "Now the fruit of righteousness is sown in peace by those who make peace" (Jas. 3:18). Peacemakers promote peace in their relationships and in how they treat of others. What a wonderful blessing!

The peace of God surpasses our ability to fully understand it, but it is a powerful guardian of our hearts as we live for Jesus (Phil. 4:6-7). What a wonderful blessing!

The God of peace will continue to bless His people with peace: "Now may the Lord of peace Himself give you peace always in every way" (2 Thess. 3:16). You can expect the Lord to bless you as you build peace into the character and conduct of your life. What a wonderful blessing!

Questions

True or False

_____ 1. Peace is a blessing from God.
_____ 2. Everybody understands what peace is and how to achieve it.
_____ 3. Sin destroys peace.
_____ 4. Once peace is destroyed it cannot be repaired.
_____ 5. God is the author of confusion.
_____ 6. The Prince of Peace will end all wars on the earth.
_____ 7. Jesus is our peace.
_____ 8. Peace rules in the Christian's heart.
_____ 9. Selfishness hinders peace.
_____ 10. Peace at all costs should describe us.

Questions for Discussion

1. Genuine peace is made up of what two things? _____

2. Define peace. What are two things that happen when peace exists? _____

3. Why do you need peace in your life? _____

4. What can you do to be a more peaceful person? _____

5. How will being peaceable help you at school, at work and at home? _____

6. Why is Jesus called the Prince of Peace? _____

7. How did Jesus preach peace according to the apostle Paul in Ephesians 2:17? _____

8. Why do you need to pursue peace when someone sins against you? _____

How can you do so (Rom. 12:17-21)? _____

_____

9. Name some ways you can be a peacemaker in your family. _____

_____

10. How do the following destroy peace?

   a. Gossip – _____

   _____

   b. Lying – _____

   _____

   c. Disobedience to parents – _____

   _____

   d. Not being thankful – _____

   _____

   e. Drinking and drugs – _____

   _____

11. Why are peacemakers called sons of God? (Matt. 5:7) _____

   _____

12. What are we told that the peace of God does for Christians in Philippians 4:6-7? _____

   _____

   Name some ways God's peace can protect you in your everyday life. _____

   _____

   _____

13. Name some peacemakers in the Bible. _____

   _____

   _____

   Why are peacemakers often not treated peacefully? _____

   _____

   _____

   _____

A Pure Heart

Lesson 9

> Building Bible character occurs in your heart. If the heart is defective, the character will not be noble.

Introduction

As a young person, you face the expectations of adulthood and the new horizons of life with excitement and enthusiasm. Life's opportunities and challenges are set before you. The instruction given you by parents, the education gained from schools and your own experiences while growing up help prepare you to be an adult. A successful life is built upon the solid foundation of a character that is in the image of Christ (Col. 3:10). This lesson is designed to help you see the value of a pure heart in building Bible character.

When advising young people on the anticipations of growing up, many tell them, "Follow your heart." Such advice may be innocent enough, but one must be careful about giving it and about following it. The Bible says, "There is a way that seems right to a man, but its end is the way of death" (Prov. 14:12). Your heart must be committed to living by the gospel of Christ and not merely by what is right in your own eyes (Judg. 21:25). You must remember that the best course for your life will not be found within you, but within the word of God (Jer. 10:23; 2 Tim. 3:16-17).

Who you are and what you will be in your life begins with your heart. The heart defines who you are: "For as he thinks in his heart, so is he" (Prov. 23:7). Building Bible character occurs in your heart. If the heart is defective, the character will not be noble. Jesus said, "A good man out of the good treasure of his heart brings forth good; and an evil man out of the evil treasure of his heart brings forth evil" (Luke 6:45). Good comes from a good heart, and evil comes from an evil heart (Mark 7:20-21).

What Is the Heart?

You will be better prepared to build the character of a pure heart by understanding what your heart really is. We all know the physical heart is the marvelous muscle that pumps blood throughout the body. But the heart we are discussing is not that at all. The Bible speaks of your heart as the seat of your thoughts and intents, your reasoning and intellectual capabilities, your emotions, your attitudes, and your conscience; your mind is your heart. Each of these areas of the heart must be purified and kept pure.

1. The heart includes your intellect. Your capacity for knowledge is because you have a heart that is made in the image of God (Prov. 23:7). Your thoughts and reasoning power exist in your heart. When you think a thought, it happens in your heart. Jesus said, "Why do you think evil in your hearts?" (Mark 9:4). When you use your reasoning ability it occurs in your heart (Mark 2:6-8). This is one of the things that distinguish human beings from animals. While animals live and survive on instinct, humans think, reason, and drawn conclusions. For example, our ability to understand is a function of the heart (Matt. 13:15). The ability to believe "from the heart" shows the intellectual ability of the heart, since belief comes from hearing the word of God and deducing that Jesus is the Christ (Rom. 10:9-10, 17). If it were not for your heart, you would have no thinking processes. We will discover that God expects us to choose to have pure thoughts.

2. The heart includes your emotions. The feelings that result from the circumstances and experiences of life are unique to human beings. Rocks and trees do not "feel," nor do animals and insects. Only humans have the ability to feel joy and pain, and all the emotions in be-

> The human conscience is a God-given monitor that informs us when we are acting in harmony with what we believe to be right (Acts 23:1; 26:9).

tween. The Bible confirms that our emotions are anchored in our heart. It speaks of "anguish of heart" (2 Cor. 2:4), of hearts that rejoice (John 16:22), of hearts that despair (Eccl. 2:20), and of hearts in distress (Psa. 38:10). The task of purifying the heart will involve making sure our emotions are right in the sight of God.

3. The heart includes your conscience. The human conscience is a God-given monitor that informs us when we are acting in harmony with what we believe to be right (Acts 23:1; 26:9). It is not our standard of right and wrong, but does help us do what we have been taught is right and not to do what we have been taught is wrong. By contrast, animals have no conscience; in the wild, they kill to survive. On the other hand, we have a moral consciousness that has been taught the sinfulness of murder. A person's heart must be cleansed from an evil conscience in order for him to draw near to God (Heb. 10:22).

4. The heart includes your will. Volition is the "act of making a choice or decision, the power of choosing or determining" (*Merriam-Webster*). You have the ability to "choose for yourselves this day whom you will serve" (Josh. 24:15). Making a choice is an action of your heart. Your motives and intentions come from your heart. The motives of your heart must conform to the word of God, because it is "a discerner of the thoughts and intents of the heart" (Heb. 4:12). Your attitudes, your decisions, your convictions, and your obedience all come from the heart (1 Cor. 7:37; Acts 2:37; Rom. 6:17). Purity of heart must include **why** you do what you do, as well as **what** you do.

Pure in Heart

Jesus said, "Blessed are the pure in heart, for they shall see God" (Matt. 5:8). The development of a pure heart is the very essence of conversion to Christ. Continuing to live in the impurity of sin is not what the Lord wants or expects of us, whether young or old (Rom. 6:1-2). Jesus expects us to be pure in heart. Otherwise, we will not see God.

David, who was a man after God's own heart, wrote, "Who may ascend into the hill of the Lord? Or who may stand in his holy place? He who has clean hands and a pure heart ... he shall receive a blessing from the Lord, and righteousness from the God of his salvation" (Psa. 24:3-5).

The apostle Paul made it plain that only those who call on the Lord out of a pure heart will please God (2 Tim. 2:22).

Because your heart defines who you are and is the origin of all that you do, it is not only important that you purify it, but also that you protect your heart from all defilement of sin. "Keep your heart with all diligence, for out of it spring the issues of life" (Prov. 4:23).

How can you purify your heart and then also keep it pure? By putting God's word deep into your heart. The psalmist wrote, "How can a young man cleanse his way? By taking heed according to your word. With my whole heart I have sought You; Oh, let me not wander from your commandments! Your word I have hidden in my heart, that I might not sin against you!" (Psa. 119:9-11).

First, you need to obey the gospel of Christ in faith and be purged from your old sins (Acts 2:38; 22:16; 15:9). The blood of Jesus Christ, who "offered himself without spot" can "cleanse your conscience from dead works to serve the living God" (Heb. 9:14). You must obey the gospel "from the heart" in order to be saved (Rom. 6:17).

Then, once you are a Christian, you must "put off the old man" of sin and "put on the new man" that is fashioned after Christ (Col. 3:9-10; 2 Cor. 5:17). It requires deliberate effort to become and to remain pure in heart.

1. To be pure in heart involves thinking pure thoughts. Since the heart includes the intellect, what we think must be pure. "Finally, brethren, whatever things are true, whatever things are noble, whatever things are just, whatever things are pure, whatever things are

> The things you read, the internet sites you visit, the music you listen to, the movies and TV shows you watch—all of these put thoughts into your heart. If impure and sinful images and ideas are allowed to come into your heart it will not remain pure.

lovely, whatever things are of good report, if there is any virtue and if there is anything praiseworthy—meditate on these things" (Phil. 4:8). This will affect some of the choices you make every day. The things you read, the internet sites you visit, the music you listen to, the movies and TV shows you watch—all of these put thoughts into your heart. If impure and sinful images and ideas are allowed to come into your heart it will not remain pure. On the other hand, by filling your mind with God's word and with good things that are honorable and noble, you will be guarding your heart against sin (Psa. 1:1-2).

2. To be pure in heart involves controlling your emotions. Just because God has given us emotions is not a good reason to fail to bring them under control. Young people are expected to purify their hearts by removing sinful emotions. The word of God commands to "be angry, and do not sin: do not let the sun go down on your wrath, nor give place to the devil" (Eph. 4:26-27). How can this be done? By being careful that our anger is righteous—directed against sin—and that we are not drawn into sin ourselves. Instead, "mediate within your heart on your bed, and be still" (Psa. 4:4). Self-discipline is required to prevent sinful emotions from corrupting our hearts. We can learn to follow the example of Jesus, who was angered and grieved by the sin He witnessed, yet who did not become a sinner. He kept His emotions under control, and so can you.

3. To be pure in heart involves keeping a clear conscience. It is right not to violate your conscience (Rom. 14:23). It is also required that you train your conscience concerning right and wrong, using the word of God as your guide. When a person commits sin and refuses to repent, his heart is gradually hardened against the will of God—his conscience is seared. If you have sin in your heart, your conscience will not continue to operate the way God intended. We must not violate our conscience if we want it to be a reliable monitor of what is right and wrong. The pure in heart endeavor to live consistently with what their Bible-trained conscience tells them in every situation.

4. To be pure in heart means conforming your will to the will of God. When your heart is fully committed to doing the will of God you will have accomplished the mental transformation described and commanded in Romans 12:2: "And do not be conformed to this world, but be transformed by the renewing of your mind, that you may prove what is that good and acceptable and perfect will of God." The mind is renewed as we deliberately choose to make God's will, our will.

Put on a Heart of...

In Colossians 3:12-15, the inspired apostle Paul wrote that Christians are to put on a heart that is different from the world; one that identifies them as the people of God. Consider how you can purify your heart with these qualities:

1. Compassion. A heart that cannot show pity on others in their time of distress is not the heart of Christ (Matt. 25:34-40).

2. Kindness. The courtesy and thoughtfulness of kindness expresses a heart that is truly interested in others (Eph. 4:32).

3. Humility. Without a humble heart one will never approach God or be blessed by Him (see Jas. 4:6-10).

4. Meekness. A heart that is strong in its convictions and at the same time controlled in its expressions of that conviction can accomplish great things. Meekness is not weakness. It combines strength of faith and self-control to do the will of God instead of the will of man.

5. Longsuffering. A heart that does not act on an impulse, that is not quick to retaliate, is like the heart of God (2 Pet. 3:9).

> A heart that is strong in its convictions and at the same time controlled in its expressions of that conviction can accomplish great things. Meekness is not weakness.

6. Forbearing and forgiving. To harbor no malice against another when wronged is the essence of forbearance. It does not overlook sin, but it seeks to overcome it through the forgiveness of Christ (Eph. 4:31-32).

7. Love. The purpose of God's commandments is "love from a pure heart" (1 Tim. 1:5). Loving God with all our heart requires a heart that is completely pure (Matt. 22:37). In like manner, we are to sincerely "love one another fervently with a pure heart" (1 Pet. 1:22).

8. Peace of God rules. We have been called by the gospel of Christ to be at peace with God and to be at peace with one another (Eph. 2:14-18). A pure heart is at peace with God, with others, and with itself.

Conclusion

Paul told Timothy to join with others who "call on the Lord out of a pure heart" (2 Tim. 2:22). A pure heart is necessary in order to follow the Lord and appeal to him for the blessings of salvation. James wrote, "Draw near to God and he will draw near to you. Cleanse your hands, you sinners; and purify your hearts, you double-minded" (Jas. 4:8). A total devotion to God is necessary in order to purify your heart.

The goal of a pure heart is to do the will of God in one's life. God described David as a man after His own heart because David would "do all my will" (Acts 13:22; 1 Sam. 13:14). We see his purity of heart when he wrote, "The statutes of the Lord are right, rejoicing the heart" (Psa. 19:8).

Young person, you can call on the Lord out of a pure heart (2 Tim. 2:22). You can have a heart that is free of "youthful lusts" and totally devoted to the will of God. The young man Daniel "purposed in his heart that he would not defile himself" (Dan. 1:8). Commit yourself to having the same purpose of heart to be pure in heart and call on the Lord.

> Young person, you can call on the Lord out of a pure heart (2 Tim. 2:22). You can have a heart that is free of "youthful lusts" and totally devoted to the will of God.

Questions

True or False

_____ 1. It is always right to follow your heart.

_____ 2. Evil things come from within and defile a person.

_____ 3. The Bible speaks of the blood pump when it speaks of the heart.

_____ 4. It is possible for the heart to think.

_____ 5. Emotions are a part of the human heart.

_____ 6. The decisions you make do not come from your heart.

_____ 7. A person can have a pure heart and not be converted to Christ.

_____ 8. What is in our hearts is shown by how we speak to others and how we treat others.

_____ 9. The pure in heart will see God.

_____ 10. Having a pure heart is not a choice you make.

Questions for Discussion

1. Explain why having a pure heart is essential to building godly character. _____
   _____
   _____

2. Why is God so concerned about the condition of your heart? _____
   _____
   _____

3. Jesus described the heart as a storehouse or treasure of either good things or evil things in Matthew _____
   12:33-37. What are some things you can do to help insure that the treasure of your heart is good?
   _____
   _____

4. Name the things that are included in the human heart (Prov. 23:7; John 16:22; Heb. 10:22; 4:12).
   _____
   _____

5. Why will the pure in heart see God (Matt. 5:8)? _____
   _____
   _____

6. What does it mean to "keep your heart with all diligence" in Proverbs 4:23? _____
   _____
   _____

7. According to Psalm 119:9-11, how can a young person purify himself and his life? _____
   _____
   _____

8. Explain why a person must obey the gospel "from the heart" in order to be saved (Rom. 6:17-18; 10:9-10). _____
   _____
   _____

9. What are some things you can do to make sure you have pure thoughts (Phil. 4:8-9)? _____
   _____
   _____

10. Name ways that you can show compassion and kindness to others (Col. 3:12). _____
    _____
    _____

11. According to 1 Timothy 1:5, what is the purpose of God's commandment? _____
    _____
    _____

12. Name some young people in the Bible who kept their hearts pure, and how they did so. _____
    _____
    _____

Lesson 10

Sound Speech

Introduction

As a young person, you are faced with the challenge of controlling your tongue so that your speech is pure. Titus is exhorted to have "sound speech that cannot be condemned" (Tit. 2:8). It is wise to be careful what we say, how we say it, and when we say it. King Solomon wrote, "He who guards his mouth preserves his life, but he who opens wide his lips shall have destruction" (Prov. 13:3). Being "swift to hear, slow to speak, slow to wrath" will keep you out of trouble as you set a good example for others. Young Timothy was taught to "be an example to the believers in word" (1 Tim. 4:12).

Your Speech Identifies Who You Are

A person's speech is an identifying trait. For example, we identify the region a person is from by the accent of his voice. The inability of the men of the tribe of Ephraim to pronounce "Shibboleth" identified them to their enemies in battle (Judg. 12:4-6). Peter's speech made it known that he was from Galilee (Matt. 26:73). Yes, your speech identifies several things about you. It is crucial that you guard your mouth and speak good things in order to develop godly character.

Your speech makes known your moral values. God's word says to *"let no corrupt speech proceed out of your mouth"* (Eph. 4:29). When something is corrupt, it is rotten and putrid. Much of the language used today fits that description. Remembering that our speech reflects the heart, you cannot expect to be "pure in heart" when your words are defiled.

Your speech makes known your spiritual values. Most people talk about what interests them. It follows that, if the gospel holds a significant part of your interest, you will talk about it to others (Rom. 1:15; 2 Tim. 2:2). Jeremiah could not keep himself from speaking in the name of God (Jer. 20:9). How easy or difficult is it for you to talk about Christ and His truth to others?

Your speech makes known your eternal values. By confessing Jesus in word and deed you proclaim your interest in eternal things (Rom. 10:9-10; Matt. 10:32-33). To be confessed by the Father we must confess Jesus here on earth.

> The tongue is extremely powerful: "Death and life are in the power of the tongue, and those who love it will eat its fruit" (Prov. 18:21).

Your speech makes known how you value others. Speech seasoned with grace will increase your opportunities to truly help those around you (Col. 4:6; Prov. 15:1-2). If you speak against others you are not showing love for them, only self-interest and contempt (Jas. 4:11-12).

Controlling the Tongue

The tongue is extremely powerful: "Death and life are in the power of the tongue, and those who love it will eat its fruit" (Prov. 18:21). Controlling your tongue means you must control your heart. It takes a lifetime of exercising self-control to keep your speech pure (1 Cor. 9:25-27). On one hand, the Bible says no one can tame the tongue; it is restless and always vulnerable to misuse (Jas. 3:8). On the other hand, the Bible teaches us that the tongue can be bridled and used in good ways by those who are spiritually mature (Jas. 3:2). You choose whether you will control your tongue and use it for good, or whether your tongue will cause harm to yourself and others.

God hears every word you speak. He will

> God hears every word you speak. He will bring your words into judgment. Jesus said, "For by your words you will be justified, and by your words you will be condemned" (Matt. 12:37).

bring your words into judgment. Jesus said, "For by your words you will be justified, and by your words you will be condemned" (Matt. 12:37). Let us consider the proper use and the misuse of the words you speak, remembering that God will judge your speech in the last day.

1. "For by your words you will be justified." Following are some examples of the sound speech that pleases God.

a. Worship and praise. "O Lord, open my lips, and my mouth shall show forth your praise" (Psa. 51:15). Expressing honor and homage to Almighty God is the essence of worship. God is seeking true worshippers (John 4:23-24). When you sing "psalms, hymns and spiritual songs," you are teaching others and honoring God (Eph. 5:19).

b. Teaching the gospel. God says the feet of those who bring the gospel to others are beautiful (Rom. 10:15). A similar description could be given to the tongue of the person who teaches God's word to others: "If anyone speaks, let him speak as the oracles of God" (1 Pet. 4:11).

c. Words of encouragement. "Walk in wisdom toward those who are outside, redeeming the time. Let your speech always be with grace, seasoned with salt, that you may know how you ought to answer each one" (Col. 4:5-6). Like salt flavors food, your words should have an influence on others to help them know and do the will of God (cf. Isa. 50:4).

d. Prayer. Whether it is thanking God for His blessings, asking for His help in your life or asking Him to help someone else, prayer is communication between you and God, between the child and his or her heavenly Father. It is a spiritual blessing enjoyed by everyone who is saved in Christ, and Christians should "pray without ceasing" (Eph. 1:3; 1 Thess. 5:17). The peace of God comforts every Christian who refuses to be distracted by the cares of this life, choosing instead to pray in every situation (Phil. 4:6-7).

e. Giving thanks. There are so many things to be thankful for, yet it is something young people (as well as old people) forget to do. Do not be one of them. "In everything give thanks; for this is the will of God in Christ Jesus for you" (1 Thess. 5:18). Take time to express your thanks to God, to your parents, to your friends, and to everyone who blesses your life. Failing to be thankful is sin.

f. Respect for others. The Lord expects us to show "honor to whom honor" is due (Rom. 13:7). As a young person, that includes the way you speak to your parents, to teachers, to adults, to your friends and peers, and to your family members. Treating others the way we want to be treated means we will use kindness and show respect in how we speak to others (Matt. 7:12).

2. "By your words you will be condemned." Here are some of the sinful uses of the tongue you are exposed to in the world and that you must devote yourself against.

a. Profanity. "Let no corrupt word proceed out of your mouth, but what is good for necessary edification, that it may impart grace to the hearers ... neither filthiness, nor foolish talking, nor coarse jesting, which are not fitting, but rather giving of thanks" (Eph. 4:29; 5:4). Profanity reveals a heart that is influenced by the flesh and by base desires. It does not take much thinking to use profane language, but it does show a sinful lack of self-control. Christians are to speak words that have a lasting good on those who hear us. Vulgar jokes and the vile words of profanity contribute nothing to the well being of the speaker or the hearer.

b. Euphemisms. A euphemism is a less offensive way of saying something, "the substitution of a mild, indirect, or vague expression for one thought to be offensively blunt or harsh" (Webster). These words are more subtle, yet just as offensive to godliness. Some of today's common euphemisms are *gee, gosh, golly, dang* and *shoot*. These words do not edify or build up; they are thoughtlessly uttered. Jesus

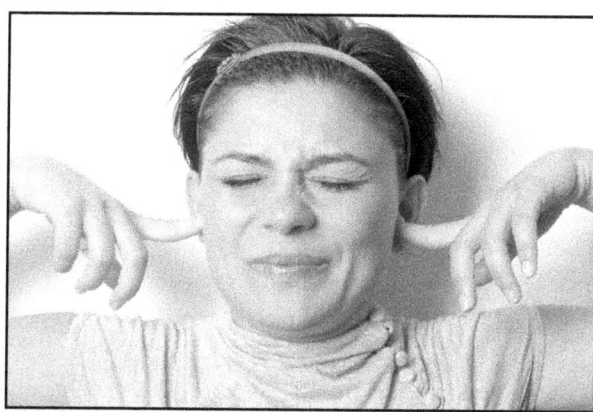

warned that we will given an account to God in the day of judgment of every "idle word" (Matt. 12:36). Euphemisms are idle, worthless words that do not bear any good fruit.

c. Lies. Telling the truth is becoming rare these days. Some people will say almost anything if they see a personal advantage in it. Lies consume the one who speaks them and can destroy those against whom they are spoken. Truth must be in our hearts. Godly character is defined by honesty and truthfulness. "Therefore, putting away lying, 'Let each one of you speak truth with his neighbor'" (Eph. 4:25).

d. Broken promises. The Christian's word is his bond. When you make a promise to someone, God expects you to keep your word (Psa. 15:1, 4). God also expects you to keep your word to him: "Do not be rash with your mouth, and let not your heart utter anything hastily before God. For God is in heaven, and you on earth; Therefore let your words be few ... when you make a vow to God, do not delay to pay it; for He has no pleasure in fools. Pay what you have vowed—Better not to vow than to vow and not pay" (Eccl. 5:2, 4-5). When you became a Christian you gave your word to God that you would follow Jesus and be like Him. To follow Jesus you must be trustworthy, doing what you say you will do. Our word should be our bond, and when we give our word, we must not break it (Mat. 5:33-37; Jas. 5:12). A man who will not keep his word is not trustworthy; he is not dependable.

e. Gossip. Gossip is idle talk, spreading rumors and bearing tales about others. Gossip may or may not be true, and can take several forms. The *backbiting* and *whispering* tongue talks behind a person's back, causing strife and conflict (Psa. 101:5; Prov. 25:23). *Slander* harms a person's influence and reputation as it reveals hatred in the heart ("whoever hides hatred has lying lips, and whoever spreads slander is a fool," Prov. 10:18; cf. Psa. 101:5). The *talebearer* circulates rumors and consequently separates friends (Prov. 16:28; 17:9). God hates "a false witness who speaks lies, and one who sows discord among brethren" (Prov. 6:19).

f. All evil speaking. The apostle taught, "Let all bitterness, wrath, anger, clamor, and evil speaking be put away from you, with all malice" (Eph. 4:31-32). Slanderous comments, angry outbursts, bitter condemnations, and malicious innuendoes—all of these and more fall under the category of evil speaking. A mouth that speaks such things reveals a heart that is immersed in self-vindication at the expense of others. Evil speaking comes from a heart that is empty of kindness, tenderness, and forgiveness.

Your goal must be to use speech that is appropriate for the occasion (Col. 4:6; Tit. 2:8). Sometimes our speech should take the form of encouragement, while at other times a rebuke will be in order (2 Tim. 4:2). There is never a time when sinful speech is proper. When you speak the truth in love, the church of Christ will be edified and your words will have a good influence on everyone who hears you (Eph. 4:15).

Conclusion

Taming the tongue and using it for good is a daily challenge and responsibility. As you develop godly character it is important that you examine your heart to be sure that godliness and holiness define who you are, because the words you speak come from your heart: "For out of the abundance of the heart his mouth speaks" (Luke 6:45). Whatever fills your heart will come out of your mouth. Fill your heart with good things like "righteousness, faith, love, patience, and gentleness" so that your words will always be honorable and acceptable to God and men (1 Tim. 6:11).

Questions

True or False

_____ 1. Sound speech can be successfully condemned.

_____ 2. Your speech does not tell anything about you.

_____ 3. The words you use reveal what is in your heart.

_____ 4. The tongue cannot be controlled.

_____ 5. Your words will not justify you before God.

_____ 6. It does not matter to God if you speak disrespectfully to others.

_____ 7. Since profanity is so common it is no longer an issue that defines character.

_____ 8. Small lies do not matter; only big lies are sin.

_____ 9. Breaking your promise shows a lack of responsibility.

_____ 10. Gossip does not hurt others.

Questions for Discussion

1. God expects young people to set an example in their speech (1 Tim. 4:12). Discuss some ways you can set an example with your words. _____
   _____

2. What are some things that your speech tells about you? _____
   _____
   _____

   Give examples. _____
   _____

3. Why is the tongue so powerful (Prov. 18:21; Jas. 3:1-12)? _____
   _____

   What must you do to control it? _____
   _____

4. What are "idle words"? _____
   How will they affect us on the Day of Judgment (Matt. 12:34-37)? _____
   _____

5. How will being careful in the words you speak help you to offer true worship to God (John 4:23-24)?
   _____
   _____

6. What does it mean that your words are to be "seasoned with salt" in Colossians 4:5-6 (cf. Isa. 50:4)? _____
_____
_____

7. Why do young people speak disrespectfully of others their age, of their parents, and of adults?
_____

   How can this be changed? _____
_____

8. What is profanity? _____
   How do you deal with the profanity you hear from others? _____
_____

9. What is a euphemism? _____
   Why are euphemisms for profanity and idle words sinful? _____
_____

10. What does lying reveal about a person's character? _____
_____
_____

11. Why is it important to keep your word or promises? _____
_____

    Must a Christian make vows in order to establish his or her honesty (cf. Matt. 5:33-37; 23:16-22)?
_____

12. Define gossip and the different forms it takes, using scriptures to support your answers. _____
_____
_____

13. Identify in Psalm 15 the good uses of the tongue and the blessings received when a person will use his words in the ways listed in this Psalm. _____
_____
_____
_____

Lesson 11

Self-Control

Introduction

Successfully building Bible character takes total commitment to faithfully follow Christ. Dedication to develop your character into the image of Christ is essential. Self-control is a key element of the character the Lord wants you to have, and is defined as the "restraint exercised over one's own impulses, emotions, or desires" (*Merriam-Webster*).

Another word used in the New Testament that is similar to self-control is "temperate"—the curbing of one's desires and impulses (see Tit. 2:2). The same word is translated "discreet" in Titus 2:5 and conveys the idea of moderation, without excess. A slightly different form of this word is used in Titus 2:6 where young men are exhorted to be *"soberminded"*—to control their passions using sound judgment.

> **Self-control begins in the heart and reveals itself in our conduct.**

Why You Need Self-Control

The apostle Paul warned against the consequences of not exercising self-control and the self-indulgent lifestyle of ungodliness: "Do not be deceived: Evil company corrupts good habits. Awake to righteousness, and do not sin; for some do not have the knowledge of God. I speak this to your shame" (1 Cor. 15:33-34). Self-control helps to protect you against the evil influences of sin.

Self-control begins in the heart and reveals itself in our conduct (see Prov. 4:23-27). Self-control is part of the fruit that is produced when one lives by the Spirit of God (Gal. 5:16-26). Without it, one will be lost.

The exercise of self-control is two-fold:

1. Self-control is needed to restrain yourself from sin and to help you choose righteous living. First of all, self-control (temperance, KJV) is necessary in order to reject temptation and avoid sin. "Each one is tempted when he is drawn away by his own desires and enticed," and "when desire has conceived, it gives birth to sin; and sin, when it is full-grown, brings forth death." The ability to master your desires and passions is critical to resisting temptation (Jas. 1:14-15). The word translated "self-control" is defined as "the virtue of one who masters his desires and passions, especially his sensual appetites" (*Thayer*, 167). Resisting the devil involves using self-control to submit to the will of God rather than giving in to sinful lusts.

Secondly, self-control is needed to help you actually do what is right. It is not enough to restrain ourselves from evil. We must also gain mastery over ourselves in order to achieve good things for God. Peter instructs us to add self-control to our knowledge of God's word (2 Pet. 1:6). As a result, self-control is the ability to govern yourself to do what you have learned. Knowing God's word without doing God's word is of no spiritual profit (Eph. 5:17; Matt. 7:21). In fact, it is sin: "Therefore, to him who knows to do good and does not do it, to him it is sin" (Jas. 4:17). By being the master over your desires and passions you are protecting yourself from evil and promoting godliness in your heart and life.

A person who does not exercise self-control will not only fail to reject sin, he will also fail to consistently choose to do the will of God. For example, consider the words you use. Sound speech excludes corrupt language (like profanity and gossip) and includes wholesome speech that encourages others (Eph. 4:29). So, you must use self-control not to speak sinfully as well as to speak good and helpful words.

> **The Duty of Self-Control**
> - Over the Spirit, Prov. 16:32; 25:28
> - Over the Life, 1 Cor. 9:25
> - Over the Lusts of the Flesh, Rom. 6:12; 1 Cor. 6:12
> - Over the Tongue, Jas. 3:2
> - Give Diligence to Possess it, 2 Pet. 1:5-7

2. Self-control helps you conform to the image of Christ. "I have been crucified with Christ" includes putting to death selfish and sinful desires so that Christ "lives in me" (Gal. 2:20). The Christian's life of sacrifice and self-control is accomplished through faith: "and the life which I now live in the flesh I live by faith in the Son of God." Without dispute, "those who are Christ's have crucified the flesh with its passions and desires" (Gal. 5:24).

By exercising self-control, the Christian will "abhor what is evil" and "cling to what is good" (Rom. 12:9).

Self-Discipline

Self-discipline is virtually the same as self-control. Every Christian is a disciple of Christ who chooses to learn and do the will of the Master (Luke 6:40). It takes discipline to do so: "Therefore, I run thus: not with uncertainty. Thus I fight: not as one who beats the air. But I discipline my body and bring it into subjection, lest, when I have preached to others, I myself should become disqualified" (1 Cor. 9:26-27; see also Heb. 12:1-2).

Paul refused to be self-indulgent because he knew that would cause him to be lost. So, he disciplined himself to do God's will. On the other hand, selfishness makes it virtually impossible to discipline and control oneself to do what is right. The selfish person is consumed with fulfilling his own desires, not the desires of God. See the lack of self-control in the following passage that describes people who have fallen away from Christ: "For men will be lovers of themselves, lovers of money, boasters, proud, blasphemers, disobedient to parents, unthankful, unholy, unloving, unforgiving, slanderers, *without self-control,* brutal, despisers of good, traitors, headstrong, haughty, lovers of pleasure rather than lovers of God, having a form of godliness but denying its power" (2 Tim. 3:2-5). People who love themselves are "without self-control"—they are governed by their lustful desires instead of by a love for God.

Applying Self-Control in All Things

Self-control is necessary in order to obtain heaven. "And everyone who competes for the prize is temperate (exercises self-control, NKJV footnote) in all things. Now they do it to obtain a perishable crown, but we for an imperishable crown" (1 Cor. 9:24-25). God promises heaven to His children, but we must take possession of our heavenly reward by faithfully doing God's will.

As we wait for the return of Christ, we must deny worldly lusts and live soberly, righteously, and godly (Tit. 2:11-12). Self-control is required every day. Here are some areas where self-control must be a part of your character.

1. Self-control must be applied to your emotions. Outbursts of anger as well as deep-seated resentment are overcome through self-control. "Be angry, and do not sin: do not let the sun go down on your wrath" (Eph. 4:26). A temper that is out of control must be brought under the control of the Spirit of God. A person who is slow to anger is wise, but the impulsive person shows himself to be foolish (Prov. 14:29).

2. Self-control must be applied to your tongue. "So then, my beloved brethren, let every man be swift to hear, slow to speak, slow to wrath; for the wrath of man does not produce the righteousness of God" (Jas. 1:19-20). The person who can control his tongue shows evidence of a mature character (Jas. 3:2). Whether it is crude jokes, profanity, or gossip, self-control will guard your tongue from sin (Eph. 4:29; 5:4).

3. Self-control must be used to be morally pure. God demands moral purity of every Christian, including young people. The grace of God teaches us to deny ungodliness and worldly lusts (Tit. 2:11-12). The following are some (not all) of the specific areas of conduct where self-control is essential to maintain moral purity

a. Sexual purity. We live in a culture that is filled with sexual immorality. Sexual activity before marriage is viewed by many people as normal and proper. Nothing could be farther from the truth. "For this is the will of God, your sanctification: that you should abstain from sexual immorality; that each of you should know how to possess his own vessel in sanctification and honor, not in passion of lust, like the Gentiles who do not know God" (1 Thess. 4:3-5). Self-control must be used to guard against promiscuous and lascivious contact before marriage. Self-control is crucial as you use the internet, where pornography and all sorts of vile images and messages exist. You must exercise self-control to *"abstain from fleshly lusts which war against the soul"* (Heb. 13:4; 1 Pet. 2:11).

b. Modest clothing. 1 Timothy 2:9-10 teaches that clothing should reveal a character that professes godliness and shows "shamefastness" (propriety, NKJV) and "sobriety" (moderation, NKJV) or "self-control" (same word, v. 15). Clothing that provocatively displays the body or fails to cover one's nakedness reveals a character that is given to the flesh and not given to godliness. God's people blush over shameful things instead of joining up with it, including the immodest clothing of the world (Jer. 8:12; Eph. 5:6-7).

c. Alcohol and drugs. Many young people view drinking alcohol as a right of passage from childhood to adulthood. In fact, it is a passage from innocence into sin and spiritual death. The word of God is clear that drunkenness, as well as the drinking that leads to it, is sin (Gal. 5:21; 1 Pet. 4:3; Prov. 20:1; 23:29-32). Your decision to no longer live "for the lusts of men, but for the will of God" will be tested by friends who will try to get you to join them in drinking parties and drug experimentation. You must have self-control to say "no" when they speak evil about you because you refuse to join with them in their sins (1 Pet. 4:4; Matt. 5:10-12).

d. Dancing. The modern dance displays an appalling lack of self-control. It incites lust and is a prelude to others sins of the flesh. The sin of lasciviousness includes the unchaste (impure) handling of males and females, something the modern dance does with abandon (Rom. 13:13; Gal. 5:19; 1 Pet. 4:3). The unrestrained, lewd, and lascivious conduct on the dance floor is set in sharp contrast to the moral restraint and moderation of self-control.

> Self-control must be used to guard against promiscuous and lascivious contact before marriage. Self-control is crucial as you use the internet, where pornography and all sorts of vile images and messages exist.

e. Gambling. Young people are increasingly becoming victims of the greed and covetousness of gambling. High school and college students are going into thousands and thousands of dollars of debt because they do not use self-control to say "no" to this destructive practice. "The love of money is a root of all kinds of

> We cannot hold evil in our hearts and bear good fruit.

evil," and gambling brings many sorrows to the person who loves money rather than God (1 Tim. 6:10). Gambling takes many forms, from the lottery to the casino. The temptation to gamble can be powerful; great self-control must be used to resist this sin's temptation.

4. Self-control must be applied to your motives. We cannot hold evil in our hearts and bear good fruit. The motives of our heart must reflect the purposes of God. Envy, jealously, malice, and bitterness are among the evil motives that we must control and overcome by crucifying "the flesh with its passions and desires" (Gal. 5:24).

5. Self-control must be used in how you treat others. Jesus teaches us to treat others like we want to be treated (Matt. 7:12). The world says "do unto others before they do it to you" (Prov. 24:29). Consider the great self-control Jesus had when He was lied about, mocked and spit on, beaten and murdered on the cross! He expects us to have this kind of self-control in how we treat others (1 Pet. 2:18-23).

Conclusion

It can be easy to put off developing self-control. Like Felix, we can convince ourselves the future is a better time to start using self-control (Acts 24:25). But, putting off the decision to obey Jesus is just another failure to exercise self-control. It is high time to wake up. Make self-control a part of our character today! Do not delay to "put on the Lord Jesus Christ, and make no provision for the flesh, to fulfill its lusts" (Rom. 13:14).

Questions

True or False

_____ 1. Self-control is a fruit of the Spirit.

_____ 2. Temperance is another word for self-control.

_____ 3. Self-control does not help you do what you know is right.

_____ 4. A Christian is never to hate anything.

_____ 5. Paul disciplined his body so he would not be lost.

_____ 6. Self-control is only useful in not becoming a drunk.

_____ 7. By controlling your tongue you show you are spiritually immature.

_____ 8. Self-control is to be added to patience according to 2 Peter 1:6.

_____ 9. Self-control cannot be shown in the type of clothing you wear.

_____ 10. Procrastination prevents many from growing in self-control.

Questions for Discussion

1. Define self-control and give another Bible word for it, and give the Scriptures that use both. ____

2. How does self-control will help protect you against the evil influences of sin (1 Cor. 15:33-34)? ____

3. What does it mean to "keep your heart" in Proverbs 4:23? ____

   How does self-control help you do this? ____

   What happens when the heart is not kept (Prov. 4:24-27)? ____

4. How is each person tempted according to James 1:14-15? ____

   Explain how self-control helps to keep a person from committing sin. ____

5. How can you know whether or not you are conformed to the image of Christ (Gal. 2:20; Col. 3:10)?

6. According to 1 Corinthians 9:24-27, how are Christians like athletes? ____

7. Using 2 Timothy 3:1-5, explain how selfishness prevents self-control. ____

8. The person who can rule his spirit is better than whom? ____

   To what is the person who lacks self-control compared (Prov. 16:32; 25:28)? ____

9. How does controlling your tongue show maturity and godly character (Jas. 3:2)? ____

How does this harmonize with James 3:8, which says no one can tame the tongue? _____
_____

10. Give some ways that you will need to use self-control when you go on a date, and explain why. _
_____
_____

11. How does immodest clothing show a lack of self-control (1 Tim. 2:9-10)? _____
_____
_____

12. Discuss whether or not smoking, drinking, and drugs help a person grow in self-control. Why not (2 Pet. 2:19; Rom. 6:12-14)? _____
_____
_____

13. Why is dancing sinful (1 Pet. 4:3; Rom. 13:13)? _____
_____
_____

14. Why is gambling sinful? _____

   Name some of the common types of gambling. _____

15. According to Galatians 5:24, what must we do because we belong to Christ? _____
_____
_____

16. Will a person be lost if he does not have self-control? _____ What is the solution to this problem (Acts 24:24-25)? _____
_____

Lesson 12

Moral Courage

Introduction

A person's character prepares him to be courageous, not only in life-threatening situations, but also in moments that challenge his faith and duty to God. That is the courage this lesson will explore from God's word—the courage to stand up for Jesus, for His truth and with His people in the spiritual warfare that we face against the greatest threat of all, sin and Satan (2 Cor. 10:3-5; Eph. 6:10-13).

What Is Moral Courage?

Building Bible character is about becoming spiritually mature. Your spiritual growth must include adding moral courage to your faith. The apostle Peter wrote, "But also for this reason, giving all diligence, add to your faith virtue, to virtue knowledge ..." (2 Pet. 1:5). The Greek word translated "virtue" means "moral excellence" and is derived from a word translated "man," so that virtue is manliness or valor concerning moral goodness and purity.

> The Lord understands it can be a fearful thing to follow him. . . . He knows it takes courage not to be ashamed of Jesus and to live a moral life.

The Lord understands it can be a fearful thing to follow Him. So, He encourages and strengthens our faith by assuring us of His fellowship and blessings in the face of the trials of faith. He knows it takes courage not to be ashamed of Jesus and to live a moral life. So, He promises, "Blessed are those who are persecuted for righteousness' sake, for theirs is the kingdom of heaven. Blessed are you when they revile and persecute you, and say all kinds of evil against you falsely for My sake. Rejoice and be exceedingly glad, for great is your reward in heaven, for so they persecuted the prophets who were before you" (Matt. 5:10-12). The blessings and promises of God convince us that we must have moral courage to say and do what is pleasing in His sight.

Why You Need Moral Courage

Sin causes fear (Heb. 2:14-15). The gospel frees sinners from the fear of sin and death. When you obey the gospel and become a Christian it is a conscious decision to serve Christ instead of continuing to serve sin (Rom. 6:16-18). Christ did not save you so you would be a fearful follower. He saved you so that you would be bold in your faith as a servant of righteousness: "For God has not given us a spirit of fear, but of power and of love and of a sound mind. Therefore do not be ashamed of the testimony of our Lord, nor of me His prisoner, but share with me in the sufferings for the gospel according to the power of God" (2 Tim. 1:7-8). Following are some reasons why you need moral courage in your life.

1. Moral courage is needed to put your faith into action. You cannot please God without faith, but we have already learned in this series of lessons that there are many kinds of faith that do not save (Lesson 6). Christians are taught to diligently add virtue (moral excellence or courage) to their faith (2 Pet. 1:5). A faith without moral purity and the courage and confidence to make moral choices is not a faith that pleases God. By faith you must have the courage to choose what is morally pure and doctrinally sound in the face of opposition and rejection, or even worse.

2. Moral courage is needed to be watchful against spiritual danger. The apostle Paul urged the Christians in Corinth to "watch, stand fast in the faith, be brave, be strong" (1 Cor. 16:13). Spiritual bravery is necessary to stand watch on the walls of your life to see the enemies of your faith that, when given a chance, will destroy your faith. The temptations to see are great and you must boldly watch against them (Matt. 26:40-41). It takes courage to "give no place to the devil" in your life (Eph. 4:27).

3. Moral courage is needed to be bold in the face of opposition. Some will mock and ridicule you for following the word of Christ and being morally pure; some will even hate you (1 Pet. 4:4; John 15:18-19). You do not need to be afraid of their attempts to discourage you and hinder your faithfulness. As you continue to live in a manner that is in harmony with the gospel of Christ you are exhorted not to be "terrified by your adversaries" (Phil. 1:27-28). "Yet if anyone suffers as a Christian, let him not be ashamed, but let him glorify God in this matter" (1 Pet. 4:16).

> Christ expects you to have a character and lifestyle that is different from the world. We are not to love the world or the things in it (1 John 2:15-17). Christians must think differently, act differently, and be different.

4. Moral courage is needed to live for heaven instead of the world. Christ expects you to have a character and lifestyle that is different from the world. We are not to love the world or the things in it (1 John 2:15-17). Christians must think differently, act differently, and be different. The tension and conflict between the truth of the gospel and the sin of the world are vividly described by Jesus in Matthew 10:34-39. There, Jesus said He brought a sword to the earth instead of peace. Those who follow Him must love Him more than anything and anyone else in the world. It takes courage to love Jesus more than family, friends, and self. But without this conviction of faith you cannot be saved.

5. Moral courage is needed to teach the gospel to the lost. The apostles of Christ preached the gospel with all boldness in the face of great opposition (Acts 14:2-3; Phil. 1:20). A similar boldness will be needed for you to talk with others about the truth. It takes courage to invite a friend to discuss the Bible with you, to visit a gospel meeting, or to attend a Bible study. Unless you have the courage to plant the seed of the gospel, your friends and neighbors and family will not hear the gospel; they will continue to be lost.

6. Moral courage is needed to be received into heaven. Jesus said, "For whoever is ashamed of Me and My words in this adulterous and sinful generation, of him the Son of Man also will be ashamed when He comes in the glory of His Father with the holy angels" (Mark 8:38). This shows us how important it is to have the courage of faith to obey His will even when we are opposed by people in the world. If I am ashamed of Jesus, I am cowardly exchanging my soul for the world and its approval (Mark 8:36-37). The cowardly will be eternally lost (Rev. 21:7-8).

Bible Examples of Moral Courage

The Bible has many examples of moral courage and faithfulness in the face of trials and opposition. We must not fail to see the blessings and rewards that their courage brought them, in life and in eternity. Here are only a few of them:

1. Noah preached a message of righteousness in a sin-filled world for one hundred twenty years—an amazing example of the persistence that moral courage requires—and was blessed with a new world, cleansed of sin (Gen. 6-8).

2. Abraham showed great moral courage to offer his son Isaac, as the Lord commanded him (Gen. 22:1-14).

3. Joseph endured tremendous trials and never failed to have the courage to do what was right (Gen. 37; 39-50).

4. Moses and Aaron had the courage to stand before Pharaoh and deliver God's message: "Let my people go!"

5. Joshua and Caleb showed moral courage by spying out the land and by declaring that Israel should go up at once and possess it (Num. 13:30; 14:6-10). They were allowed to enter the promised land while the rest of their generation died in the wilderness.

6. Daniel and his companions refused to compromise their convictions before the powerful king and were blessed with positions of favor and honor (Dan. 1:6-20).

7. The apostles faced continual persecutions yet successfully spread the gospel throughout the world (Matt. 28:18-20; 1 Cor. 4:9-13).

Traits of Moral Courage

It is possible to identify some common traits of moral courage that will help you develop this worthy trait within your character.

1. Proper priorities. Moral courage seeks first the kingdom of God and His righteousness (Matt. 6:33). It will not put selfish interests or pleasing men before pleasing God (cf. John 12:42-43).

2. Unwavering commitment to God. Daniel and his Hebrew companions had an extraordinary commitment to the law of God (Dan. 1:8-20; 3:16-18; 6:7-10). It rose above a commitment to the law of King Nebuchadnezzar and above a fear for their personal safety.

3. Trust that God's ways are always right. Faith is key to moral courage. By trusting that God's word is always right, the courageous Christian will obey the Lord regardless of the cost to himself (Heb. 11:33-38).

4. Refusal to compromise. Whether pressed by men to compromise with moral corruption or doctrinal error, moral courage will not yield to the pressures applied against it (2 Tim. 4:2-5). It will be watchful not to be deceived by the subtleties and temptations of sin (1 Pet. 5:8; Jas. 1:14-16).

Things that Hinder Moral Courage

1. Fear of men (peer pressure). Jesus said His disciples must not be afraid of men who can only kill the body (Matt. 10:28). One of the greatest pressures that hinders and prevents moral courage is peer pressure. The pressure to be like the world in your attitudes, words, and conduct can become great, yet Jesus says "do not fear these things" (Rev. 2:10). You must be committed to moral excellence and have the courage to put that commitment into practice. True character will not hypocritically claim to be committed to moral purity but practice immorality.

The solution to peer pressure is given in Proverbs 1:10-16; 4:14-19 and Psalms 1:1-2. Refuse to consent with sinners and completely reject their attempts to draw you in to sinning with them. Listen to the wisdom of God's word and just say "no"!

> **Examples of Moral Cowardice**
> - Herod, Mark 6:14-29
> - Pilate, Luke 23:1-25
> - Peter, Luke 22:54-62
> - Believers who would not confess Jesus, John 12:42-43
> - The Sanhedrin Council, Acts 4:13-22
> - Felix, Acts 24:22-27

2. Fear of being isolated. Everyone wants to be accepted by others, to be liked by others and to have friendships with others. Some will go along with sin because they do not want to stand out or be different. Jesus does not teach you to avoid people in the world. However, when you choose to be a faithful Christian, there will be people who will insult you and reject you (1 Pet. 4:12-14).

The solution to this fear is, rather than be discouraged, remaining bold and confident to keep on doing the will of God. People may reject you but the Lord never will. "So we may boldly say: The Lord is my helper; I will not fear. What can man do to me?" (Heb. 13:6)

3. Fear of the cost of being faithful. There is a price to be paid for being a Christian. Some are unwilling to pay the price and sacrifice themselves fully to Jesus (Luke 14:26-36). And, some Christians will not pay that price, either. The cost of losing friends, family, fame, or fortune in order to obey Christ is too great for them. And so, they cowardly shrink into the shadows so no one will know they are a Christian. But, the Lord sees this cowardice (cf. Peter, Luke 22:60-62).

The solution to fearing the cost and sacrifice of discipleship is to remember the great cost God paid to save you. The death of the Son of

> ... worldly, weak and disobedient Christians discourage the hearts of their brethren.

God assures us that we are more than conquerors through Him. "What shall we say to these things? If God is for us, who can be against us?" (Rom. 8:31-39). Nothing and nobody is greater or mightier than God. Therefore, have courage and faith to trust Him. Have the courage to follow Him.

4. Fearful, faithless Christians. Perhaps the most damaging discouragement of all comes from other Christians who will not faithfully follow the will of God. Like the fearful Israelites who discouraged their brethren, worldly, weak and disobedient Christians discourage the hearts of their brethren today (Deut. 1:26-28).

The solution is to strengthen your faith so that you do not discourage others. Instead, live in such a way that your brethren take courage from you and are made stronger when they see your life. Always remember that "he who is in you is greater than he who is in the world," and be brave! (1 John 4:4; 1 Cor. 16:13).

Questions

True or False

_____ 1. A Christian does not have to be concerned with being afraid to follow Jesus.

_____ 2. Choosing to be morally pure is included in moral courage.

_____ 3. Moral courage must be added to faith in order for one's faith to please God.

_____ 4. Only elders and preachers need moral courage to teach others.

_____ 5. A lack of moral courage will not cause a person to be lost.

_____ 6. Moral courage is needed when one's faith is tested by sin and error.

_____ 7. Peer pressure includes the desire to please those who know us.

_____ 8. Setting spiritual priorities has very little to do with developing moral courage.

_____ 9. It is okay for you to go along with your friends when they are sinning.

_____ 10. God should be feared more than any person.

Questions for Discussion

1. What is moral courage and where is the word used in the New Testament? _____
_____
_____

2. Why do you need moral courage? _____
_____
_____

3. Explain why moral courage must be added to your faith in order for your faith to grow and be pleasing to God (2 Pet. 1:5; 1 Pet. 5:8-9). _____
_____
_____

4. According to Revelation 21:7-8, what will happen to those who are moral cowards? _____
_____
_____

5. Name some things that can hinder moral courage and the solutions for each one. _____
_____
_____

6. According to the following passages, what can you do to overcome peer pressure?

Moral Courage

a. Proverbs 1:10-16: _____

_____

_____

b. Proverbs 4:14-19: _____

_____

_____

c. Psalms 1:1-2: _____

_____

7. Name three young men in the Bible who risked their lives to be faithful to God, and give the scripture that tells their story. _____

_____

_____

8. Why did it take courage for Joseph to say "no" to Potiphar's wife? _____

_____

_____

9. Your friends are planning a drinking party Friday night and want you to come along. You tell them you don't drink, but they say come along anyway. How will you answer? Why? _____

_____

_____

10. Another young person who is a Christian is planning to go to the school dance and wants you to go, too. What should you do? What will you do? _____

_____

_____

11. Your friends are telling filthy jokes at school. How do you react? _____

_____

_____

12. Using Romans 8:31-39, give reasons why every Christian should live courageously and not be discouraged by people and circumstances of life. _____

_____

_____

Lesson 13

Self-Sacrifice

Introduction

This series of lessons has presented building blocks for constructing Bible character in your life. The task of building your character into the image of Christ is not easy and will not happen without personal effort and commitment. The cost you will have to pay to build godly character is high. The cost will not be measured in currency, but in the sacrifices you make in order to put the Lord and His will first in your life (Phil. 3:7-11).

Jesus taught a great deal about the cost of discipleship. A key element of being a disciple of Christ is self-sacrifice. To follow Jesus you must deny yourself everything that would keep you from being saved and from doing the will of Christ. Jesus said, "... whoever of you does not forsake all that he has cannot be My disciple" (Luke 14:33). This final lesson is about making the necessary sacrifices in order to shape and mold your character into the image of Christ (Luke 6:40; Col. 3:10).

Self-Sacrifice

"Sacrifice" is defined as "the act of offering; then, objectively, that which is offered" (*Vine*, 543). From the days of Abel onward, humans have brought offerings to God (Gen. 4:4). The Law of Moses commanded many animal sacrifices to be offered by the priests for the people of Israel (Heb. 10:1-4). Today, Christians serve as priests in the house of God (which is the church of the living God) and offer up "spiritual sacrifices" to God (1 Pet. 2:5). Just as the sacrifices of the Old Testament law were to be offered to God according to His prescribed will, the sacrifices we offer to God must also be according to what has been revealed in His word (Heb. 8:5; Col. 3:17).

1. The Christian's sacrifice is voluntary. "Your people shall be volunteers in the day of your power" (Psa. 110:3). The Son of God has all power at the right hand of God, and Christians willingly offer themselves to Him. Your obedient service to the Lord cannot be forced upon you; it is freely given by everyone who intends to be saved and mature in Christ.

2. The Christian sacrifices his life to Christ. "I have been crucified with Christ; it is no longer I who live, but Christ lives in me; and the life which I now live in the flesh I live by faith in the Son of God, who loved me and gave Himself for me" (Gal. 2:20). Your faith is a sacrifice that is offered to God (Phil. 2:17). Your decision to be a Christian is a decision to completely surrender (offer, sacrifice) yourself to the Lord. Your sacrifice must be complete or the character you build will not be upon the solid rock (Matt. 7:24-27).

3. The Christian sacrifices his body to Christ. "I beseech you therefore, brethren, by the mercies of God, that you present your bodies a living sacrifice, holy, acceptable to God, which is your reasonable service" (Rom. 12:1). It is completely inconsistent to allow your body to be "washed with pure water" and then use it to serve the impurities of sin (Heb. 10:22). As a Christian, you are no longer a slave of sin; you serve the Lord Jesus Christ. Therefore, your body is to be offered in service to God to do what is righteous in His sight (Rom. 6:6-14). The character you are building is committed to obeying the will of God in all things by using your body to accomplish that obedience (Rom. 6:15-18; 1 Thess. 4:1-8).

4. The Christian offers sacrifices of praise to God. "Therefore by Him let us continually offer the sacrifice of praise to God, that is, the fruit of our lips, giving thanks to His name" (Heb. 13:15). God's people willingly and joyfully worship the Lord according to His will (John 4:24).

5. The Christian offers the sacrifices of goodness and sharing with others. "But do not forget to do good and to share, for with such sacrifices God is well pleased" (Heb. 13:16).

When you do something good for another person you are following God's example of love (Matt. 5:44-48). Offerings of kindness to relieve the needs of others are consistent with the character of God. The Lord will reward the merciful and compassionate treatment of others (Matt. 25:34-40).

> ... when you sacrifice yourself to Christ it will cost you everything; but the price you pay is worth it!

The Character of Self-Denial

Sacrifice is not free; it comes at a price. King David said he would not offer to God that which cost him nothing, so he purchased animals and the place of sacrifice (2 Sam. 24:24). He surrendered something of value in order to worship God. Similarly, when you sacrifice yourself to Christ it will cost you everything; but the price you pay is worth it!

1. Self-denial is essential to salvation. Without it, one lives in the selfishness of sin. "If anyone desires to come after me, let him deny himself, and take up his cross daily, and follow me. For whoever desires to save his life will lose it, but whoever loses his life for my sake will save it. For what profit is it to a man if he gains the whole world, and is himself destroyed or lost?" (Luke 9:23-25). It is not enough to "desire" to follow Jesus; one must "deny himself" and bear the burden required of him actually to be a follower of Jesus.

2. Self-denial imitates Jesus. His life was one of self-sacrifice and self-denial. From emptying himself of the glory of heaven, to the lowly station He occupied on earth, to the shameful treatment at the hands of sinners and His death on the cross, Jesus is the fullest expression of self-denial. Christians willingly bear the reproach of Christ in order to reign with Him in glory (Heb. 13:13; 2 Tim. 2:10-13).

Sacrificing personal wants and wishes in order to be saved eternally is at the heart of being a Christian. Remember, Jesus said, "... whoever of you does not forsake all that he has cannot be My disciple" (Luke 14:33). A popular spiritual song announces, "All to Jesus, I surrender, all to him I freely give; ... I surrender all." Let us be sure such total surrender describes who we are. Here are some of the things self-denial freely surrenders in order to be a disciple of Christ.

1. Self-denial surrenders self. Selfishness is a hindrance to godly character. Earthly wisdom encourages and displays "self-seeking" as the way to get ahead and to achieve success in life (Jas. 3:14-16). However, selfishness never satisfies the soul and always generates additional trials and trouble. The sin of selfishness must be put away from your heart in order to have godly character.

2. Self-denial surrenders the sins of the past. The sins of the past cannot be changed, but they can be forgiven and no longer practiced.

> **Things Jesus Sacrificed**
> - Heaven's glory, Phil. 2:5-8; 2 Cor. 8:9
> - High station, Matt. 2:23
> - Earthly comfort, Luke 9:58
> - Honor of men, Psa. 22:6-8
> - Justice, Acts 8:33
> - Life, John 10:17-18

"This I say, therefore, and testify in the Lord, that you should no longer walk as the rest of the Gentiles walk" (Eph. 4:17-19). The willingness to put away all the sins of the past is a mark of conversion and character of the person who has chosen to live for Christ (Col. 3:5-10; 1 Pet. 4:2-3).

3. Self-denial surrenders the values of the world. The world is under the influence of Satan, but Christians submit to the authority of Jesus (1 John 5:19; Matt. 28:18-20). Your new life in Christ involves changing your values and priorities from those of the world to those that conform to the will of God (Matt. 6:33). "For what profit is it to a man if he gains the whole world, and loses his own soul? Or what will a man give in exchange for his soul?" (Matt. 16:26).

4. Self-denial surrenders everything that hinders faithfulness. Jesus clearly taught that every obstacle to faithfulness must be removed:

"If you right eye causes you to sin, pluck it out and cast it from you; for it is more profitable for you that one of your members perish, than for your whole body to be cast into hell" (Matt. 5:29). Paul said, "What things were gain to me, these I have counted loss for Christ" (Phil. 3:7). Whether it is a destructive friendship, a sinful activity or an evil association—nothing can be allowed to keep you from doing the will of God.

Practicing Self-Sacrifice

The Bible says that the person who practices righteousness is righteous (1 John 3:7). Likewise, we cannot just talk about self-sacrifice; we must practice it every day. Self-sacrifice that is not practiced is no sacrifice at all!

1. Self-sacrifice is necessary to repent and be saved. The godly sorrow that produces repentance unto salvation is ready and willing to sacrifice every sin that was previously committed (2 Cor. 7:10; Acts 19:18-20).

2. Self-sacrifice is necessary to worship God. Many excuses are heard from those who choose not to deny self and worship the Lord as He has commanded. To put the Lord first and worship Him will mean sacrificing your time and your personal convenience to assemble with God's people (Acts 20:7; Heb. 10:24-25). Giving as the Lord has prospered you involves self-sacrifice (1 Cor. 16:2; 2 Cor. 9:6-7).

3. Self-sacrifice is necessary to learn God's word. Time and effort are required to study and learn the Bible. The upright in heart will sacrifice whatever is necessary in order to learn and live the word of God (Psa. 1:1-2; 25:4-5; 2 Tim. 2:15).

4. Self-sacrifice is necessary to live a moral life. The gospel calls us to put away evil companions and immoral conduct (2 Cor. 6:14-7:1; 1 Tim. 6:11; 2 Tim. 2:22). As you live in the world you must not be of the world (John 17:15-17). That requires putting away every desire of the flesh and putting on the Lord Jesus Christ (Rom. 13:13-14; 1 John 2:15-16).

5. Self-sacrifice is necessary to help those in need. To have the ability to help someone in need but refusing to do so does not show the love of God (1 John 3:17-18). It is not the character of Christ (Matt. 25:35-41).

Conclusion

Sacrifice characterizes true disciples of Jesus. The disciple's purpose in life is to "gain Christ"—everything else is secondary to that goal. "But what things were gain to me, these I have counted loss for Christ. Yet indeed I also count all things loss for the excellence of the knowledge of Christ Jesus my Lord, for whom I have suffered the loss of all things, and count them as rubbish, that I may gain Christ" (Phil. 3:7-8). The Christian who is shaping his character into the image of Christ will not allow anything to keep him from following Jesus; not inconvenience, not time, not physical discomfort or any other condition and consideration.

The Lord promises wonderful blessings to those who forsake all and follow Him. "Then Peter began to say to Him, See, we have left all and followed you. So Jesus answered and said, Assuredly, I say to you, there is no one who has left house or brothers or sisters or father or mother or wife or children or lands, for My sake and the gospel's, who shall not receive a hundredfold now in this time—houses and brothers and sisters and mothers and children and lands, with persecutions—and in the age to come, eternal life" (Mark 10:28-30).

As a young person, your life is set before you. You have many opportunities and advantages ahead of you. Remember, the greatest and most rewarding course of life will be to always put the will of God first. "But seek first the kingdom of God and His righteousness, and all these things shall be added to you" (Matt. 6:33).

> . . . we cannot just talk about self-sacrifice; we must practice it every day. Self-sacrifice that is not practiced is no sacrifice at all!

Questions

True and False

_____ 1. Some things must be forsaken in order to be a disciple of Christ.

_____ 2. Sacrifice is the act of receiving something from another person.

_____ 3. Sacrifice is commanded, yet voluntary.

_____ 4. The person who is crucified with Christ hangs on a cross.

_____ 5. Christians are living sacrifices.

_____ 6. Jesus did not have to practice self-denial.

_____ 7. Selfishness prevents self-denial.

_____ 8. Everything that prevents faithfulness to Christ must be removed.

_____ 9. It does not take much sacrifice to be saved.

_____ 10. Self-denial must be practiced, not just preached.

Questions for Discussion

1. In Luke 14:25-27, Jesus makes it clear who cannot be His disciple. Who cannot be His disciple? _____

2. In that same passage Jesus teaches us to count the cost of discipleship (Luke 14:28-33). What does this mean? _____

3. What is a sacrifice? What did David say about the cost of a sacrifice to God? Give scripture. _____

4. What did Jesus sacrifice for you? _____

   Discuss similar sacrifices you should make for Him. _____

5. Discuss the sacrifices a Christian offers to God, giving an example of each one. _____

6. What does it mean to take up your cross when you follow Jesus (Luke 9:23)? _____

7. According to 1 Peter 4:1-4, what must you surrender in order to be a Christian? _____
   _____

8. Discuss the type and the extent of self-sacrifice that must be made from the following passages:

   a. Phil. 3:4-11: _____
   _____

   b. Col. 3:5-10: _____
   _____

9. What will self-sacrifice for Christ cause you to do in the follow situations?

   a. Your friend wants you to join him or her in drinking alcohol. _____
   _____

   b. It is time to go to Sunday morning Bible classes and worship, but you are very tired from being out late Saturday night. _____
   _____

   c. You have a job and you must choose between giving to the Lord and spending it all on yourself. _____
   _____

   d. You have a Bible class lesson to prepare, but you keep putting it off. _____
   _____

   e. You know what you need to do to obey God, but if you do it your family will reject you. ____
   _____

10. Why do you need to spend time learning the Bible (Psa. 19:7-13; 2 Tim. 2:15; 1 Pet. 3:15)? ____
    _____
    _____

11. In Matthew 6:24-34, Jesus made it clear that we cannot serve two masters. According to this passage, _____ why should we seek first the kingdom of God and His righteousness? _____

    How do you do this? _____
    _____

12. What will a person receive who forsakes all and follows Jesus (Mark 10:28-30)? _____
    _____
    _____

www.ingramcontent.com/pod-product-compliance
Lightning Source LLC
Chambersburg PA
CBHW080942040426
42444CB00015B/3409